What Readers Are Saying About
Live Inspired

"In *Live Inspired*, Shirley masterfully weaves together stories from her life with the biblical narrative in such a way that, as a reader, you are drawn in. She is funny, relatable, and authentic all at once. *Live Inspired* helped me grasp grace in a way that my achievement-driven nature wouldn't always allow."

—Benjamin Hutchins, MRE,
Pastor of New River Valley Church, Blacksburg, VA

"Shirley's words and raw vulnerability took me through an engaging and enlightening journey in better understanding what it looks like to whole heartedly pursue overcoming performancism. Even after knowing Shirley for a couple years, this book gave me deeper insight into the brilliant, God-fearing woman that she is. If you're looking for a book filled with inspiring scriptures, personal real-life examples, and stories of people from the Bible brought to life, this is the one for you!"

—Natalie Gregory, Campus Ministry Leader,
Greater Pittsburgh Church of Christ, Pittsburgh, PA

"Vulnerable. Practical. Biblical. This is the book we didn't know we needed. Shirley invites the reader into her own journey through an often-underplayed topic and maps out a journey from misguided drive to the empowered life God intended."

—Jon and Lindsay Landis, Evangelist and Women's Ministry Leader,
Roanoke Valley Church, Roanoke, VA

"Shirley takes the reader with her by the hand on an active and progressive journey from the awareness of our self-driven tendencies—and their underlying cost—to the free and more enjoyable life meant by God. Very well documented with research and a thorough analysis of the Scriptures, this didactic book is also punctuated by numerous highly personal stories we can deeply relate to. This remarkable combination makes us willing to embark wholeheartedly on this transforming adventure—head, heart and soul."

—Armelle Neboit, Chief accountant at Nestlé and Author of "Job de Cœur", a blog dedicated to Christians in the workplace

Live Inspired offers realistic biblical truths to search as you work on living a spirit-led life. These biblical truths are helpful as you work on practical ways to overcoming the self-driven life, to living spirit filled. I really enjoyed Shirley's honesty along with her struggles on how God works in our lives daily, encouraging us to grow stronger in Him. In reading her book I am continually encouraged that God wants us to *Live Inspired*."

—Teresa Linner, Retired Elementary School Teacher, Pahrump, NV

"Shirley Desmond Jackson's book, *Live Inspired: Freeing Ourselves from the Grip of Performancism*, is a breath of fresh air for all of us overachievers and perfectionists. It's a comforting hug of understanding yet a challenging call to grow into grace."

—Eni Szabad, Student at Radford University, Radford, VA

"In *Live Inspired*, Shirley has creatively and accurately captured the nature of being driven by performancism. At times, it felt like she looked into our hearts and minds and expressed what has often been an ambiguous enigma of feelings and thoughts. This book is a must read for all of us who have ever struggled with the feelings of paralyzing fear of failure and finding self-worth in the rigid and merciless system of results only oriented thinking. This work has given us a vocabulary and framework to use to aid in our own journeys of growth and living a Spirit-led, inspired life."

—Delano and Nadine Stewart, Evangelist and Women's Leader,
Valley Christian Las Vegas, NV

"I have enthusiastically believed in this book from its first edition to this newly expanded version. *Live Inspired: Freeing Ourselves from the Grip of Performancism* clearly and concisely walks with readers in the direction of freedom. The unexpected treasure to unearth in this book is the richness of a deeper relationship with God along with the added blessing of learning and being encouraged to rely more on the Holy Spirit. The encouragement to practice active memorization of scripture and times of silence and solitude is incredibly valuable for daily living. With deep insight, raw vulnerability, and biblical truths to bolster each chapter, the goal of becoming stronger in the Spirit began to enrich my life from the first chapter to the finish. This superb book is a gift to all readers who wish to live inspired through the love and grace of Jesus Christ."

—Jody Rohleder, Administrative Accountant RE/MAX Northwest,
Westminster, CO

Published by Market Refined Publishing,
An Imprint of Market Refined Media, LLC
193 Cleo Circle
Ringgold GA 30736
marketrefinedmedia.com

Print ISBN: 979-8-9903602-6-6
Digital ISBN: 979-8-9903602-7-3
Library of Congress Control Number: 2024920007

Cover and Interior Design by Nelly Murariu at PixBeeDesign.com
Manuscript Edits by Market Refined Media, LLC

Printed in the United States of America

Second Edition: October 2024

Live Inspired

Freeing Ourselves from the Grip of Performancism

Shirley Desmond Jackson

*This book is dedicated to all who know
the crippling pain of a self-driven lifestyle.
May the truths in God's Word lead you
to the freedom of a Spirit-led life.*

*"Jesus said, "If you hold to my
teaching, you are really my disciples.
Then you will know the truth, and
the truth will set you free."*

John 8:31b–32

Contents

Introduction   xiii

Chapter 1: Seeking Spirit-Led Truths   1

Quiz: What Kind of Achiever Am I?   12

Chapter 2: Grasping Grace   19

Chapter 3: Favoring Failure   33

Chapter 4: Sifting Success   47

Chapter 5: Aligning Allegiance   61

Chapter 6: Building Boundaries   77

Chapter 7: Easing Expectations   91

Chapter 8: Cultivating Collaboration   105

Chapter 9: Letting the Spirit Lead   117

Live Inspired Bible Study Companion   131

Acknowledgments   133

About the Author   137

Notes   138

Introduction

Sitting with my circle of friends, I bared my soul. From anyone else's perspective, I had it all: a thriving career, supportive marriage, healthy children, great friends, and a connected church community. Yet I was miserable. I'd always been highly-motivated and driven to succeed, but anxiety and stress robbed me of any joy. I struggled to believe this was the abundant life Jesus promised to His followers.

As I exposed my inner angst, the other women looked at me with compassion. But no one shared words of wisdom. We all knew our lives *should* be marked by peace and joy. Instead, we each felt frazzled, frustrated, and forlorn. Adding to our distress was the conviction that somehow, we were to blame. If we could only figure out the formula, we could enjoy our lives.

Every Christian career woman wants to know how to balance her driven nature with the life of grace and peace Jesus promises. Too often our outward appearance of success and achievement masks the inner turmoil of our hearts and souls. We appear confident, but we are instead drowning in self-doubt. Our inner voice acts like a tyrant who pushes us relentlessly. We believe working harder will solve the problem, but it just makes us more tired.

When success doesn't come with more work, we look for spiritual answers. We read books about overcoming perfectionism and people-pleasing, but nothing carries enough power to completely silence the drive of our inner voice.

My struggle led me to research what it means to be a self-driven achiever, and I discovered the inner angst and turmoil I felt pointed to a deeper issue. The problem is *performancism*—we tie our identity and self-esteem to our performance and accomplishments. At some point, when we were young, we learned to identify ourselves and our value by what we could achieve. Most of us don't even realize how strong that connection truly is. As we grew, we developed strongholds, or deeply-held convictions, which continue to trap us in the grip of performancism today.

The key is to identify and replace them with a Spirit-led focus. This book will help us break free from the grip of performancism by exchanging our self-driven practices for a Spirit-led life. This is where we will find the peace and joy we want but have struggled to achieve.

We will begin by examining Satan's lies and the strongholds they created in our lives. Next, we will challenge these lies with the truths found in God's Word. Spiritual disciplines and practices will help us tap into the power of the Holy Spirit, and each chapter will conclude with reflective questions designed to help us personalize the content. We will also receive encouragement to dig deeper into the Word for His truths.

After reading this book, you will discover why you became a self-driven achiever and how to break its bonds. You will face hard truths along the way, but Jesus promises these truths will set you free (John 8:32). You'll also learn time-tested spiritual disciplines, or practices, to guide you in your journey. With God's help, this book will lead you to inspiration and freedom.

So, let's imagine we are sitting together in a quaint and quiet sidewalk cafe. As we settle in with our coffee or tea, we begin to share our hearts. Friend, this is where your journey from self-driven bondage to Spirit-led freedom begins.

CHAPTER 1

Seeking Spirit-Led Truths

"The Lord does not look at the things people look at. People look at the outward appearance, but the Lord looks at the heart." 1 Samuel 16:7b

That morning, like so many others, the four of us congregated in one of the corners of the spacious staff room. Of the twenty new hires at the international accounting firm, we were the only women. Instinctively we banded together.

Each of us came from different socioeconomic backgrounds and ethnicities, yet we shared the same drive and work ethic. After earning our place in the firm, we looked forward to fulfilling our career goals and dreams. Our impromptu morning meetings became a source of encouragement and support as we faced the challenges of working in the real world.

One colleague immediately stood out. Beautiful, talented, and accomplished, Jade exuded confidence. And for good reason. Not only did she carry an impressive resume of achievements, but she also radiated warmth and kindness. The three of us felt drawn to her. We didn't just want to be her friend—we wanted to *be* her.

But soon the strain began to take its toll on Jade. With rare and raw vulnerability, she shared with me her secret pain caused by crippling anxiety. She dreaded disappointing others and struggled to meet the expectations she placed on herself. Her career with the firm had barely started and she already wanted to quit. This strong and vibrant woman began to crumble before my eyes. Unable to manage her stress, she left the firm prematurely.

What I could see so clearly in my friend I failed to recognize in myself. We both suffered from performancism—we tied our identity and self-worth to our achievements. This unchecked need to achieve, or to perform, fueled our self-driven natures.

What Does It Mean to Be a Self-Driven Achiever?

The term "self-driven" isn't found in conventional dictionaries but is commonly thought of as being *personally motivated to achieve goals*. A self-driven person is often described as self-motivated, determined, or tenacious.[1] It follows that self-driven achievers are people who push themselves to achieve their goals.

On the surface, the description of self-driven achievers appears positive and desirable. Their motivation, drive, and ability to succeed never fail to impress. So much of what they do is not wrong; in fact, it's often highly praised. But beneath the outward signs of success and accomplishment, we find a different story. We see the struggle and hidden costs that come from it.

When I follow my self-driven instincts, I perfect the art of appearing calm, cool, and collected. People often compliment me on what they see as my "quiet and gentle spirit" (1 Peter 3:4). But that's only because I learned to hide the chaos that constantly churns inside my head and heart.

Every time I take on a project, professional or personal, my immediate and overwhelming emotional response is fear.

- If I'm preparing an oral presentation, I fear falling flat on my face.

- If I'm working on a project, like writing an article or organizing an event, I'm afraid I won't produce a quality product.

- No matter what I'm doing, I worry I will disappoint others.

- And I always fear I won't live up to the reputation I've earned through previous achievements.

As a Christian, I feel an added pressure. People noted Jesus did everything well (Mark 7:37). Ultimately, I fear letting God down by not holding to the same standard of excellence.

Together these hidden fears forge a nervous energy that I've learned to channel toward the task at hand. This is when I develop what my husband calls *tunnel vision*. My thoughts and actions are consumed with not failing. Pushing past all reasonable boundaries for rest or sleep, I cajole myself with thoughts like, "The world is run by tired people."

Any requirement to work with others adds another layer of stress. Because I can't force other people to adhere to my high standards, I end up doing more to make up for their lack. Resentment soon follows.

But it's the people I love the most who receive the brunt of my inner fury. Their needs become my impediments or distractions. I end up frustrated with their timing. Can't they see how busy I am? Can't they wait until I'm done with this project? (Although they would argue that I am never done.) Without fail, my impatience spills over with harshness. I snap with irritation and bark orders.

Finally, when the task is completed, I feel either relief or disappointment, but never joy. But only for a moment. Then the cycle repeats.

The self-driven achiever's true nature does not paint a very pretty picture. And it certainly fails to depict a quiet or gentle spirit. While all mask the internal turmoil of their heart and soul, their internal struggle may take different forms. Some self-driven achievers, like Jade, display signs of perfectionism. Others, like me, become overachievers. Let's take a closer look at each of these types of self-driven achievers.

Overachiever or Perfectionist?

On the surface, overachievers and perfectionists look alike because they both set high standards for themselves and work exceedingly hard to meet them. To understand the difference, we have to look deeper—at their motivation.

The following table highlights these differences:

OVERACHIEVERS	PERFECTIONISTS
Driven by an overwhelming fear of failure.	Driven by a need for perfect results.
Try to overcome their low self-esteem by avoiding failure.	Try to earn their worth through perfect results.
Do more than what is necessary to avoid failure.	Push themselves to achieve perfect results.
Success brings feelings of relief because they didn't fail.	Success brings disappointment when the results are less than perfect.

To complicate matters further, overachievers can define failure as a lack of a textbook outcome. When this happens, perfectionist tendencies kick in. As they strive for flawlessness, perfectionists can push themselves to overachieve. The following Venn diagram illustrates this overlap:

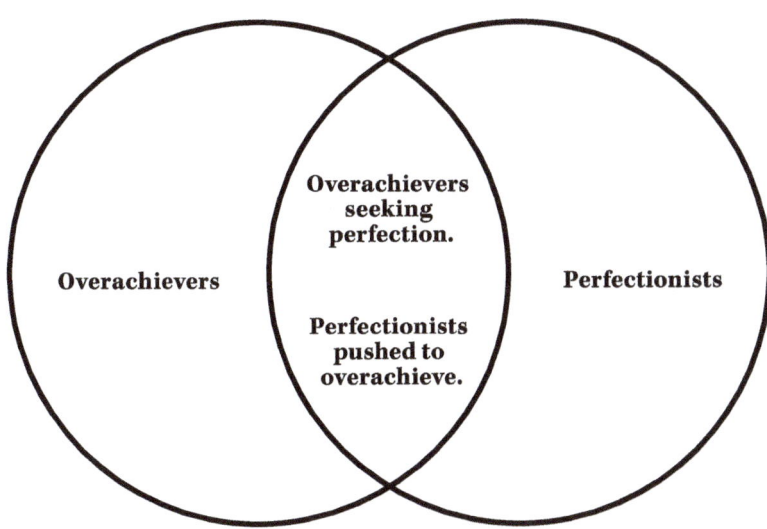

Regardless of being an overachiever or a perfectionist, the end result is the same. Both are self-driven achievers and struggle with performancism because they tie their identity and value to their performance and accomplishments. The pressure they put on themselves to achieve creates stress and robs them of their peace and joy.

What about you? Are you beginning to think of times when you can see yourself as a self-driven achiever? Maybe you...

- Hold yourself to an impossibly high standard.

- Feel haunted by your fear of failure. It invades your thoughts and takes your emotions captive.

- Hesitate to share your feelings, especially your insecurities and fears.

- Struggle to control the drive to achieve and watch helplessly as your physical or spiritual health suffers from exhaustion.

- Know the pain of crippling anxiety.

- Find yourself teetering on the brink of burnout.

- Long for the reassurance that God is pleased with you just as you are.

If so, you are not alone. Let's look at the seven key characteristics that all self-driven achievers—whether a perfectionist or an overachiever—share:

1. **Self-doubt:** Self-driven achievers lack self-confidence, so we use achievements to conquer our self-doubts and validate our worth.

2. **Fear of failure:** Failure is seen as a final judgment that diminishes our value.

3. **Focused on results:** Only the end result counts. We rarely enjoy the journey.

4. **Tendency toward people-pleasing:** Craving the approval of others, we often compromise our integrity and dreams to please others.

5. **Inability to say "no":** We consistently overextend ourselves by taking on extra work. We easily become workaholics and often sacrifice our personal lives to meet work demands.

6. **Unrealistic expectations:** We frequently set unrealistic and rigid expectations for ourselves. In order to meet them, we push ourselves, and others, with harsh words and behaviors.

7. **Trouble trusting others:** Working in groups sets us on edge. We fear other members won't share our work ethic and will cause us to fail.

Each of these characteristics are rooted in lies from Satan. These lies form strongholds–deeply held beliefs or convictions—that fuel the self-driven lifestyle and keep us bound to performancism.

Together we will tackle these strongholds and learn how to dismantle them. But first, let's look at how God wants us to live by seeing what happens to these beliefs when we become a Spirit-led achiever. Here are seven key characteristics to consider:

1. **Self-confidence:** Our self-worth and confidence do not depend on our ability to achieve. As Spirit-led people, God's love defines our worth and His grace gives us the confidence we need.

2. **Acceptance of failure:** We see failure as a tool to help us grow. We don't necessarily like failure, but we don't fear it either.

3. **Enjoy the journey:** We want to meet our goals, but we realize how well we progress toward the goal is also important. We know how to enjoy the journey.

4. **Pleasing God:** Although we want to be likable, we realize we will not always be liked. Being Spirit-led means we align our allegiance with our Heavenly Father and do not try to win the favor of people.

5. **Healthy boundaries:** By setting appropriate boundaries, we enjoy all aspects of our lives.

6. **Realistic expectations:** When we're Spirit-led, we know what we can realistically accomplish given our skill set and resources. We avoid the trap of overextending ourselves.

7. **Invite collaboration:** We have learned goals are best met when people collaborate. We encourage others' participation and input.

Did you notice how the Spirit-led achiever has shifted her perspective? Where is her confidence anchored? How has she redefined failure and success? What healthy lifestyle choices does she now make? The strongholds created by the lies of Satan have been dismantled and she is free to embrace God's truths. As a Spirit-led achiever, she has learned how to experience peace in her journey and joy in her accomplishments.

The Spirit-led life is our goal. But when you think about what needs to change, you may feel overwhelmed. This may be the first time you realized how many of the self-driven strongholds are present in your life. It can be hard to see ourselves as we are, especially when we don't like what we see.

Let's take comfort in this truth from God's Word. *"The Lord does not look at the things people look at. People look at the outward appearance, but the Lord looks at the heart"* (1 Samuel 16:7b). The beautiful reality is that God has always seen our hearts which reflect our true selves. He is not surprised at what we now see, and He has a vision for our transformation. God knows we long for the Spirit-led life and is waiting to lead us to it.

At the beginning of my journey, I needed to work on every one of those self-driven characteristics. If that's you too, take heart! The key to shifting our perspective is replacing self-achieving strongholds with the truths of God's Word. Seeking and implementing these Spirit-led truths will be the core of our work together. Each time we demolish a stronghold, we loosen the grip of perfomancism. We'll see that these changes don't happen overnight, but we'll also discover we don't have to do it in our own power either. God has given us everything we need through the Holy Spirit.

The Ultimate Goal: Relying on the Holy Spirit

In his second letter to Timothy, Paul encourages him with these words, "For the Spirit God gave us does not make us timid, but gives us power, love and self-discipline" (2 Timothy 1:7). Timothy had many reasons to be timid. He was young for an evangelist, he had frequent illnesses, and he lived in a world where Christians were severely persecuted. But Paul reminded him that the Spirit gave him everything he needed to follow God's plan for his life: *power, love,* and *self-discipline.*

We may face different challenges than Timothy, but we have the same promise from the Holy Spirit. The Greek word translated as "power," *dunamis,*[2] describes the ability to perform, or accomplish. Interestingly, our word, *dynamite,* is derived from the same root. Imagine the power of a stick of dynamite at our disposal. The Spirit's power is strong enough to demolish the strongholds of our self-driven ways.

The Greek word translated as love in this passage is *agapé.*[3] We correctly think of love as an emotion. But the word agapé also communicates the idea of love expressing itself through action. Jesus reminds us that if we love Him, we will obey His commands (John 14:15). Obedience doesn't come easily, so Jesus immediately promises to send us a helper, the Holy Spirit (John 14:16-17). With the Spirit's help, our love for Jesus will motivate us to obey His truths rather than Satan's lies.

The lies we've believed have grown deep roots in our hearts, minds, and characters. As we challenge them with God's truths, we may feel a sense of *cognitive dissonance.* This is the uncomfortable feeling of recognizing two opposing points of view. In these moments we will have a choice: will we continue to believe the lie, or will we exchange it for the truth? Here is where the Spirit's third gift of self-discipline will come into play.

The Greek word translated as self-discipline is *sóphronismos.*[4] As used in this passage, it literally means to choose behaviors that follow God's will and wisdom. We all know how difficult it can be to break a bad habit. The Spirit will give us the discipline to not only demolish our self-driven characteristics but also replace them with sound practices that align with God's will.

As we move forward, know that Jesus loves you right where you are. He will gently lead you in this journey, just as He did me.

Pressing on Toward the Goal

What kind of achiever are you? Take the quiz at the end of this chapter and find out. Spend some time in prayer, asking the Holy Spirit to help you see where you might display self-driven achiever tendencies. Then grab your favorite pen and journal your answers to the following questions:

- What have I learned about myself?

- What do I hope to achieve by reading this book?

- Which of the self-driven characteristics resonate most with me?

- Which of the Spirit-led characteristics do I long for?

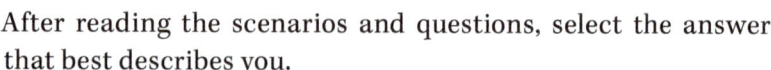

QUIZ — What Kind of Achiever am I?

After reading the scenarios and questions, select the answer that best describes you.

Scenario 1

Your supervisor has tasked you with organizing refreshments for an event she is hosting. The event will be an outreach opportunity to showcase the work your organization is doing in the community. The budget is small, so she suggests asking members of the organization to contribute enough food for both the members and several guests. Because the event is open, a specific headcount cannot be determined.

Question 1: Although the event is open to all, the supervisor is asking every member to bring at least one guest. Since the event is to be held midmorning, you decide to serve a selection of savory and sweet items. To assign the treats each member should bring:

- *Answer A*: After determining how many treats each member should bring, you create a sign-up sheet for them to complete on a first-come, first-served basis. They can freely choose between savory or sweet.

- *Answer B*: After determining how many treats each member should bring, you carefully delegate assignments so there is an equal distribution of savory and sweet, and enough variety in each category.

Question 2: As the event draws to a close, a member of the organization who is also a professional caterer approaches you. Surveying the leftover food, she notes the remaining treats are the perfect quantity—not too many, nor too few. Everyone had their fill, and nothing was wasted. In response:

- *Answer A*: You breathe a sigh of relief. All the hard work has paid off.

- *Answer B*: Thank her for her insight and ask how she liked the event overall.

Question 3: Just as the professional caterer walks away, your supervisor approaches you. Surveying the food remaining on the banquet table, she points out certain items are completely gone. She is concerned some attendees were unable to sample everything. Your response:

- *Answer A*: Deflated, you apologize, promise to do better next time, and leave as soon as possible.

- *Answer B*: You share the observations of the caterer and ask your supervisor for her thoughts.

Scenario 2

Your schedule has been very busy for the last few weeks. You've put off working on a gift you are making for your mother's birthday. You finally have a free evening and look forward to catching up on your project. But before you can get started, a friend invites you to a little get-together at her house. It sounds like fun, but your mother's birthday is coming up soon. When you explain your situation, she encourages you to bring your project and work on it during the get-together.

Question 4: Weighing the options, you make your decision:

- *Answer A*: You express your regrets and ask to take a rain check. You spend your evening finishing your mother's gift as originally planned.

- *Answer B*: You accept your friend's invitation and take your project to the party. But the lively conversation distracts you. Unable to focus, you make some mistakes. Even though everyone assures you the gift is beautiful, you still see the flaws. You go home frustrated and stay up late so you can fix it.

Scenario 3

You are attending a mandated professional training for your career. The packet you received includes two lists of articles to read. One list is required; the other one is recommended.

Question 5: You have limited time to prepare for the training so you:

- *Answer A*: Cancel other plans so you can read the articles on both lists.

- *Answer B*: Only read the articles on the required list.

Question 6: During the training, you are assigned to work with people from other organizations. As you share your thoughts, another participant disrespectfully dismisses them.

- *Answer A*: You thank the participant for her viewpoint but let her know how her response made you feel. You ask her to stay professional in future interactions.

     Answer B: You cringe and feel defensive. You either stop sharing your thoughts or try to adjust them so you won't incur any more disapproval from this participant.

Scenario 4

Your supervisor asks you to be part of a task force to complete a new project for your organization. The work involved does not align with your wheelhouse of skills, nor do you share your supervisor's passion for it.

Question 7: You decide to:

     Answer A: Share your reservations and limitations with your supervisor. After clarifying expectations, you agree to serve on the task force. Even though you don't share your supervisor's passion for this particular project, you do believe in the overarching mission of the organization.

     Answer B: You feel honored that your supervisor selected you for this task force and immediately join. Besides, you've always been a model employee, and you want to protect your reputation.

Question 8: When you are assigned your responsibilities in the group, you:

     Answer A: Procrastinate because you are worried you will let everyone down. You don't want to start until you know you can produce the right result. Then you hunker down and do whatever is necessary to complete your assignment with excellence.

   Answer B: Enjoy learning something new. You work diligently but make sure to respect your personal needs for rest.

Question 9: You notice one of the task force members is not meeting her responsibilities. You:

   Answer A: Worry about her noncompliance and how it will affect the project overall. Frustrated, you remember this is why you hate working in a group.

   Answer B: Speak with your colleague to determine what is causing the problem. After hearing her side of the story, you offer suggestions for how she can resolve the issue and still fulfill her responsibilities.

Question 10: Which of the following mantras best describes your work ethic?

   Answer A: Work is only one necessary and integral part of life.

   Answer B: Work first, play later.

Tabulate your results by circling your answers to each question in the following table. Calculate how many responses are in each column.

If the majority of your responses are in the Self-Driven Achiever column, this book is written for you. We will address specific strongholds and challenge them with biblical truths.

If the majority of your responses are in the Spirit-Led Achiever column, congratulations! You are where we all want to be. This book will still prove valuable. We often find it difficult to teach others anything we do naturally. The principles in this book will help you empathize with self-driven achievers and give you the tools to help them grow.

If the majority of your responses are split between the Self-Driven and Spirit-Led columns, you still have some strongholds that tie you to performancism. Keep reading to discover where you follow your self-driven tendencies and how to free yourself of them.

QUESTION	SELF-DRIVEN ACHIEVER	SPIRIT-LED ACHIEVER
1	B	A
2	A	B
3	A	B
4	B	A
5	A	B
6	B	A
7	B	A
8	A	B
9	A	B
10	B	A

CHAPTER 2

Grasping *Grace*

*"Let us then approach God's throne of grace
with confidence, so that we may receive mercy
and find grace to help us in our time of need."*
Hebrews 4:16

Trying to hide my nerves behind a bright smile, I took the seat offered to me. A colleague had arranged this interview with a French accounting firm. On it I had pinned all my hopes—this job could finance my dream to live in Paris and support the planting of a church there.

"And you speak French?" he asked with some skepticism.

"Oh yes," I quickly affirmed, "I've studied it for a few years in college."

Immediately the interview switched to French, exposing the inadequacy of my language skills. I could not understand his questions, let alone respond intelligently. The conversational

French I learned in college did not include any professional business terminology.

After an eternity, the interview ended. I did not get the position. Numerous job interviews met with the same disappointment. My lack of language skills disqualified me from most jobs. To be able to stay in France, I finally accepted a position as an *au pair* (nanny).

It wasn't only my professional life that suffered, my personal life did too. Before moving to France, I often volunteered for my church by leading individual and small-group Bible studies. I had hoped to do the same in Paris.

But I quickly learned that language is a habit—we tend to use the same words over and over. My college French trained me to discuss literature or the weather but left me unable to teach the Bible or speak about Jesus. I even struggled to communicate with the children I nannied. Navigating my life in France often left me feeling less capable than a five-year-old.

I had trained with my church for three years so I could serve on this mission team. But nothing prepared me for how inadequate I suddenly felt. Losing my abilities—both professional and personal—left me feeling completely worthless. For the first time, I realized how deeply my self-esteem depended on what I could do.

Building Self-Worth Through Achievements

Building our self-worth through our abilities or accomplishments is one of the most defining characteristics of a self-driven achiever. To a certain extent, almost everyone living in contemporary Western culture identifies themselves by their professions. One of the first questions we ask when meeting someone new is, "What do you *do*?"

But while everyone builds some of their self-esteem through what they do, the self-driven achiever relies almost exclusively on their achievements for validation. It could be that we are born with a more driven personality than others. Then as we grew, and others praised our efforts, we began equating our value with what we could achieve. Somewhere along the way, we began to believe this lie from Satan: *I am only worth what I can produce.* And we develop our stronghold that states: *I will build my self-worth and self-confidence through my achievements.*

For me, this process started very early. I knew how to read before I started school. My teachers immediately labeled me as a *proficient student.* Their praise encouraged me to study hard and earn high grades. Soon I began to be known as the *honor student.* Later my drive and work ethic caused me to be known as the *highly effective employee.* It worked in my personal life as well. I became the *tireless volunteer,* the *helpful friend,* the *wise spiritual mentor.* Every part of my identity tied to something I could do.

How about you? Can you see where what you did began to define who you are? Maybe you always loved working with children. You became the *child whisperer.* Or you loved organizing social gatherings, so you became known as the *event coordinator.* Excelling in your profession, you became identified as the *expert* in your field.

The self-worth we build through our achievements is short-lived. Ultimately, we will begin to believe we've lost value if we are no longer able to perform as expected. This is what I faced during those first few months in Paris. Since I could no longer communicate effectively, hold a job in my field, or serve the church in a familiar capacity, I felt completely worthless.

Tying our identity to the temporary value of our achievements also undermines our confidence. While our achievements should make us feel secure, we actually drown in self-doubt. Each task becomes a new challenge to prove ourselves and a new possibility to fail. Our self-esteem rises or falls according to our most recent performance, so we continue to believe the lie that we can build our self-worth and confidence by achieving more. But the lie never satisfies our needs. It only blinds us to the truth. God's grace alone has the power to fulfill our longing for value and identity. The only way for us to break this cycle is to replace Satan's lie with God's truth. Let's look at how this works.

God's Truth

Many of my young friends, as well as my daughter, recently became first-time moms. Their newborns need constant attention and care, like around-the-clock feedings, diaper changes, burps, and snuggles. These babies can give nothing in return for the sacrifices of their mothers, yet they are loved for no other reason than for who they are: *their mother's child.*

I've loved watching all these moms with their babies. But my eyes filled with tears as one shared her unique testimony. Adopted as a young child, she never knew her biological parents. All her life my friend wondered about her physical and personality traits—where and from whom did she get them? Now, as she looks at her daughter, she sees someone who looks like her—someone who has her sweet smile, her button nose, and her sparkling eyes. She has a deeper appreciation for what it means to be made in the image of God. Her testimony reveals such a simple, yet powerful truth.

God always planned for our identity to be rooted in our relationship with Him. When He created us, He lovingly made us in His image. You might say God gave us His DNA (Genesis 1:27). He meant for us to reflect His glory as we lived in communion with Him. But somewhere along the way, each of us has sinned or done things that caused us to fall short of His expectations (Romans 3:23). To restore us to our intended relationship with God, Jesus bore the consequences of our sins through His sacrifice on the cross (1 Peter 2:24).

Not only did Jesus' sacrifice rescue us from our sin, but it also clarified our identity. Galatians 3:26 says, "So in Christ Jesus you are all children of God through faith." Simply put, we are daughters of the King. Our identity remains fixed, nothing we do, or don't do, can change this truth. Our identity comes not from what we do, but who we are. Or rather, *Whose* we are. And God loves us for no other reason but that we are His children. There is yet another layer to Jesus' sacrifice, however—it settled the question of our value.

In my training as an accountant, I learned to determine an item's value by how much someone is willing to pay for it. If you have ever bought or sold a house, you have seen this in action. A house may be listed for a certain amount, but the final value is only determined after the buyer and seller negotiate. The amount the seller is willing to accept, and that the buyer is willing to give, defines the house's value. So how does this help us to understand our value?

The apostle Peter explains it this way, "It was not with perishable things such as silver or gold that you were redeemed from the empty way of life handed down to you from your ancestors, but with the precious blood of Christ" (1 Peter 1:18–19a). In Greek, the word translated as *redeemed* is *lutroó¹*. It means to release by paying a ransom. On the cross, Jesus released us from our sins and opened the way for us to become God's children. But it cost Him everything—His very life. We can also look at this from the Father's perspective. He values us so much that He willingly exchanged the life of His Son for our freedom.

It doesn't matter how unworthy we *feel*. The price paid for us— *the lifeblood of Jesus*—determines our value, or worth. And just as we saw with our identity, this value never changes. It was paid once and for all time. We can neither increase it with our good deeds nor decrease it with our bad ones.

The above paragraphs are a simplified version of what we think of as God's grace. If you are familiar with the Bible or have been around church settings, this information isn't new. But since you are reading this book, I suspect that you, like me, struggle with fully understanding grace. Not in the *I-don't-know-what-it-means* way, but in the *how-do-I-accept-and-respond-to-it* way.

God's Gift of Grace

The word often translated as "grace" in the New Testament comes from the Greek word, *charis²*, and is defined as God's unmerited favor toward man. Grace can refer to any of God's gifts to us, but we most often link it to our gift of salvation. Understanding grace as a gift is not as simple as it appears. Definitions of gifts, as well as the social conventions surrounding them, differ by individuals and cultures. To fully grasp the nature of grace, we need to understand how our culture, as well as our personality, shapes our understanding of gifting.

In contemporary Western culture, gifts help us create and foster relationships. The gift's value expresses how we feel about the relationship. By definition, gifts are meant to come without strings attached.[3] But this has not been my experience. Self-driven achievers don't feel worthy of a string-free gift. So for us, a gift represents what some sociologists refer to as a social debt.[4] We feel obligated to repay the gift to maintain the status of our relationship. At the same time, our overthinking nature causes even more anxiety. We don't want our gift to offend or to send the wrong message.

This is how it plays out for me. When someone gives me a gift, I feel obligated to give one back. I try to reciprocate with gifts of equal value so I can maintain equality in my relationships. A more expensive gift risks embarrassing the other person. A gift of lesser value shows a lack of appreciation for our relationship.

What about you? Do you struggle with the social conventions of gifting? Maybe you have experienced the discomfort of receiving an unexpected gift. Did you wonder if the gift signaled a shift in your relationship? To keep your relationship balanced, you may have felt compelled to dash out to the store and buy something for the giver. I developed a habit of purchasing and wrapping extra gifts at Christmastime so I could be prepared for these "gift emergencies."

Or maybe you find unreciprocated gifts leave you feeling indebted to the giver. I once had a colleague who brought me a tasty treat once a week from a specialty coffee shop. My offers to pay for them went unheeded. I'm sure she offered these gifts without any strings. Even so, I always felt like I owed her something.

This whole cycle of giving and reciprocating gifts is exhausting. We tally the gifts we've received against those we've given, and we strive to keep it all balanced. Keeping this "gift scorecard" prevents us from focusing on what is really important—enjoying the gift of our relationships. And we are the ones who ultimately lose.

When I apply my understanding of gifting to my relationship with God, I see similar patterns. Through Jesus, God offers me the incredible gift of salvation. But accepting it creates a social debt and I feel obligated to offer Him a gift of equal value. I do this through my obedience and good works. Everything between God and me is fine—until I miss the mark.

When I fail to live up to God's standards, my thoughts begin to follow a familiar pattern of faulty thinking. I believe my gift to Him loses its worth, signaling that I don't value our relationship. Displeased, I imagine God begins to pull back His gift of grace, so I offer renewed obedience and good works. It's a vicious cycle where I am always trying to be better, so His grace flows to me again.

Do you find yourself engaging in this frustrating dance of gift reciprocation? Like me, you would never say you are trying to earn your salvation. We know this is impossible. We also know we don't have the means to return His grace with a gift of equal value. But reciprocating gifts helps us self-driven achievers feel less unworthy.

On the other end of the spectrum are those who freely accept gifts without feeling the need to give back. Have you ever wondered if they have a better grasp of God's grace? To answer that question, we need to consider the culture of gifting which existed during the time of Jesus' ministry.

Gifting in Ancient Roman Culture

Gifting also played a big role in Ancient Rome, but its social meaning and implications were very different. The Romans had no social infrastructure to care for the less fortunate, so they developed a system of reciprocal gifting to provide for those in need.[5] Through this system, people in need (clients) formed special relationships with the people who had the means to help them (patrons).

This is how it would have played out if I couldn't provide for my needs. I would find a person who could supply what I lacked and ask him to engage me as a client. If he accepted my request, he became my patron, and we entered into a life-long relationship. I always knew my place. Clients never assumed equality with their patrons.

My patron's benevolent acts increased his social status. The social norms of Roman culture expected my patron to fulfill his obligation to me. In the same way, as his client, I was expected to honor his generosity with loyalty and small acts of service. As long as we both met our cultural expectations of patronage, our cycle of reciprocal gifting would continue.[6]

It was in this culture that Jesus came and delivered God's gift of grace. This means the first recipients would have looked at it through the lens of patronage. Let's see how the author of Hebrews describes this relationship:

> "Let us then approach God's throne of grace with confidence, so that we may receive mercy and find grace to help us in our time of need." Hebrews 4:16

The hierarchy of the relationship remains clear. God, as our patron, sits on a throne, and we, His clients, are subordinate to

Him. But God's throne is a throne of *grace*. To approach with confidence means we can freely, yet respectfully, present our needs to Him. As our patron, God has already agreed to help us. So, we also have confidence in knowing He will provide whatever we need. In return, God expects us to honor His gifts by remaining loyal and devoted to Him.

Before I understood the patronage relationship, I thought the only righteous way for me to approach God would be to grovel at His feet, confess my sins, and promise to do better. Only then could I hope to receive God's gift of grace.

What about you? Have you seen how your feelings of unworthiness influence the way you approach God? Maybe you hope He will choose to help you, even though you don't feel worthy of it. The best you can do is try to minimize your unworthiness by doing your best to live up to His standards of righteousness. So you, like me, tried to build self-esteem and confidence through your accomplishments. But God knocks our carefully constructed stronghold over and flips it on its head.

When God is our patron, our relationship isn't based on our *unworthiness* and His ability to love us anyway. It's based on our *inadequacy* and His willingness to provide for our needs *because* He loves us. Understanding this truth leads us to build *holy confidence.*

Building Holy Confidence

As self-driven achievers, we tried to overcome our self-doubts through our achievements. We hoped to come out on the other side feeling confident. But this type of confidence is rightly called self-confidence because it is built on us. Instead, we need to focus on building *holy confidence*—one that is built on the truths of God's Word. The path to this confidence begins by accepting and embracing the following truth:

I am both worthy and inadequate.

Our worth, as we discussed above, has been permanently fixed by the price Jesus paid for our souls. But knowing our worth won't erase our feelings of inadequacy. Deep down we all know we are incapable of earning our salvation, eternal life, or even providing for many of our daily needs, like oxygen. Only God can meet them all. When we stop trying to hide our inadequacies or overcompensate for them, they will lead us to a greater dependence on God, our patron. Our confidence will come, not from our achievements, but from God's promise to provide what we need.

As you read this you may be feeling that sense of cognitive dissonance we discussed earlier. It's the uncomfortable feeling of holding two contradictory beliefs. For so long we've pushed ourselves to achieve so we can feel valued and gain confidence. How do we suddenly stop? The short answer is we don't—it takes time. Our self-achieving habits run deep, and it will take some effort on our part to change them. But remember, we don't have to do this alone. We can partner with the Holy Spirit.

The first step is to *choose* to believe the truths in God's Word. We may be tempted to skip over this step and think it isn't necessary. But when we're faced with a truth from God's Word which contradicts one of our deeply held beliefs, our prayers need to become gut-wrenchingly honest.

Lord, I don't know how it is possible to find my worth and identity in You alone. But because Your Word says I can, I am choosing to believe it. Please help me through Your Holy Spirit to live this truth out in my life. Amen.

One way the Spirit helps us is through the meditation of scripture. For example, let's try meditating on Hebrews 4:16. Imagine the scene. As we approach God's throne of grace, we can picture His open, receptive posture. He is waiting for us to lay our needs before Him. Not just some, but *all* our needs: big, little, physical, emotional, spiritual, professional, and material. There is absolutely nothing we can't place before Him. We can see Him nodding and agreeing to help us. As we lift our eyes to the throne, we are reminded of His sovereignty. We realize He may meet our needs differently than we expect. But because it is a throne of grace, we trust He will ultimately choose what is best for us.

Next, we can lean on the Holy Spirit's discipline to memorize scripture which define our identity and worth through the lens of God's grace. Whenever we're tempted to return to a self-driven mindset, the Spirit will pull these verses from our memory and remind us of His truths.

We can also engage in the practice of solitude and silence. This is a special prayer time that we can practice during our daily quiet time or whenever we feel a disruption in our joy or peace. To engage in this prayer, we take time to sit with the Lord, away from distractions. We silence the voices around us, including our own. We assume a posture of surrendering and listening. We surrender our doubts, our plans, and our need to prove ourselves through achieving. Then we pray to accept the truths of our identity and worth. Finally, we ask the Spirit to help us find the answers to questions like the following:

- Where am I trying to earn my worth from my achievements?

- What needs or lacking should I lay before the throne of grace?

- In what ways am I relying on myself rather than on God?

The Spirit's answers don't always come immediately. Sometimes new insights happen as we return to mundane everyday tasks, like emptying the dishwasher or walking our dog. Other times they come through a sermon, a thoughtful social media post, or a timely conversation with a spiritual friend. But they do come. The key is to be waiting, watchful, and willing to listen.

As we understand and accept God's truths about our identity and worth, we will be able to stop neutralizing our doubts through our achievements, and we will stand with *holy confidence*. Not a confidence constructed with the temporary currency of our accomplishments, but one built on the permanence of our relationship with God. A confidence no longer built on ourselves but on the holy truths of God's Word.

As we replace Satan's lie with His truth, we loosen the grip of performancism and demolish our self-driven stronghold of relying on our achievements. In its place stands our new, Spirit-led conviction: *I will grasp God's grace and love as the determination of my identity and worth and stand with holy confidence.*

Pressing on Toward the Goal

The practical implications of grace can be difficult to grasp. Take some time to process this chapter's content by sitting with the Holy Spirit. Ask Him to help you answer the following questions:

- How have my cultural expectations of gifting influenced my understanding of God's gift of grace?

- The path to confidence lies in accepting and embracing the following truth: *I am both worthy and inadequate.* How can this help me with my confidence?

- What do I still need to understand about grace?

Research additional scriptures on grace. Write out the ones that resonate with you the most. To get you started, here are a few of my favorites:

- "For God so loved the world that he gave his one and only Son, that whoever believes in him shall not perish but have eternal life. For God did not send his Son into the world to condemn the world, but to save the world through him." John 3:16–17

- "Do not be afraid, little flock, for your Father has been pleased to give you the kingdom." Luke 12:32

- "He who did not spare his own Son, but gave him up for us all—how will he not also, along with him, graciously give us all things? Who will bring any charge against those whom God has chosen? It is God who justifies. Who then is the one who condemns? No one. Christ Jesus who died—more than that, who was raised to life—is at the right hand of God and is also interceding for us." Romans 8:32–34

CHAPTER 3

Favoring Failure

"For though the righteous fall seven times, they rise again, but the wicked stumble when calamity strikes." Proverbs 24:16

Staring at the circled number written in red ink, I felt a warm flush creep across my face and neck. I had never failed a test in my life. Yet the score—42%—could not be clearer. Despite my diligent study efforts, I failed the exam. As my heart raced, my thoughts exploded in a thousand different directions.

"How did this happen? What went wrong? The aptitude tests I took in high school must be wrong. Clearly, I'm not cut out for a career in accounting. What am I going to do? How do I tell anyone . . . everyone I failed? I need to switch majors. What are the possibilities? Hotel and Restaurant Management? No, there's a high failure rate in that industry. Business Administration? Possibly. I need to see a counselor when this class is over. Will I lose credits? How much will it cost me to switch majors? I've invested so much in this dream. How can I change course now? But I have no choice. I failed."

In the background, my professor's voice droned on and on as he meticulously reviewed the exam questions. I only half-listened as my mind continued to search for a solution to my problem. Suddenly my ears perked up when he offered to share the grading curve with us.

As I watched him write the curve on the board, I breathed a sigh of relief. My score, the second highest in the class, equated to a "B." Technically, I failed the test. But so had everyone else. I received grace that day and no longer felt it necessary to switch career paths. But that close brush with failure, along with some others along the way, shook me to my core and haunted me for years to come.

The Cost of Failure

Everyone fears failure to a degree. But for the self-driven achiever, this fear takes on a life of its own. It directly sabotages our attempts to build our worth and identity through our performance. The intense blow to our self-esteem leaves us doubting we can recover. So we easily believe this lie from Satan: *Failure is a final judgment that diminishes my value.* And we build our stronghold which states: *I will avoid failure at all costs.*

In the last chapter, we clarified the truth about our identity and self-worth. But embracing these truths won't immediately erase our fear of failure. There are nuances to this fear that we need to expose and replace with God's truths. As I thought about why I fear failure, I saw it was really the consequences I hated so much. Specifically, I fear losing the following:

- **Loss of respect:** As a self-driven achiever, I crave that others see me as competent and intelligent. Failure threatens the respect people have for me.

- **Loss of relationships:** I hate to disappoint others. When I fail the people in my life, I worry they will stop trusting me. Depending on the severity of the failure, I risk damaging the relationship or losing it altogether.

- **Loss of resources:** I always invest my time, money, or effort in any task I undertake. Failure means I may not get any return on my investment.

- **Loss of opportunities:** I always fear any failure will close the door to future opportunities.

The pain of failure intensifies when it causes loss in more than one of these areas. Failing that exam jeopardized my reputation as one of the strongest accounting students at my university. It also threatened my relationship with my parents who expected me to do well. Because of these potential losses, I almost walked away from what later became a successful career in accounting.

That failure pushed me to double, or even triple, my study efforts. Since I never failed another exam, I believed success demanded this type of effort. I began to apply the same work ethic to other parts of my life.

How about you? Do you see ways you overthink and overdo to avoid failing at something? Or maybe your fear of failure causes you to shrink back from taking risks and trying something new. Both are common ways for us to avoid the pain of failure. But these are learned responses.

Think about when children first learn to walk. They don't show this fear of failure. They do fall, and sometimes the fall catches them by surprise. Other times it scares or hurts them. But they don't lose heart. Young children are naturally resilient. They persevere until they succeed. So how and when did we learn to fear failure?

Why We Fear Failure

Demanding authority figures is one of the main reasons we learn to fear failure. The opinions of parents, teachers, or coaches influence us greatly, especially in our formative years. Their criticisms, even if well-intended, begin to shape our feelings toward failing.

In the fourth grade, I won a school-wide essay contest which granted me a personal meeting with the governor of our state. I remember asking my father if he was proud of me. "Yes," he conceded, "I'm proud of you when you do things like this. But I'm disappointed in you when you fight with your brother." With that, he left the room, and not another word was spoken. From other conversations, I know my father was proud of me and my accomplishments. But I still can't think of that moment without feeling the same sense of loss. For years I believed no success could ever offset my failures. So, I resolved to never fail.

How about you? Do you see ways critical people influenced your feelings about failing? Maybe you, like a friend of mine, had highly successful parents. For her, only high As, not even an A-, were allowed on her report cards.

Or maybe your athletic or musical talents brought you under the authority of coaches. Another of my friends is a gifted pianist; however, the demeaning criticism of her mentor destroyed her confidence.

Shame and guilt enter our hearts and souls when those we trust and respect won't accept our shortcomings or give us vision for growth. Although these emotions look and feel the same, they are actually very different. Shame tells us we are a bad person. But guilt tells us we've done a bad thing (or failed to do a good one). How we interpret our mentors' criticisms determines which of these emotions we feel. In either case, we begin to associate these feelings with failure.

Trauma, especially when we can relate it to a time we messed up, also teaches us to fear failure. This trauma can be anything from simple embarrassment to the devastating loss of a relationship.

In middle school, I absolutely dreaded my PE class, and not just because I wasn't good at it. Every day we played volleyball. And every day I found myself on the team with the class bully. I can still see her, looking over her shoulder and threatening me to hit the ball... *or else.* When I missed (which I almost always did), she rushed over, got in my face, and threatened bodily harm. She couldn't do anything in class, but I always feared she would catch me in an unsupervised area and make good on her threat.

The fear I associated with failing in volleyball carried over to other areas of my life. That middle-school bully lived long in my memory and constantly warned me not to fall flat, be it on an exam, in a relationship, or in my job... *or else.*

Can you see ways trauma has led to your fear of failure? Maybe you flubbed up a presentation and suffered ridicule and scorn as a result. Or you didn't meet the expectations of your employer and lost your job and livelihood.

Because of the embarrassment, humiliation, or intense loss associated with these events, we learned to fear failure of any kind. Thankfully, we don't have to stay stuck there. We can conquer it when we look at failure from God's point of view and adopt His perspective.

God's View of Failure

When we read through the scriptures and observe how God responds to the failures of His people, we can see He operates with a growth mindset. I first learned about the role of mindset through the work of Dr. Carol Dweck, a professor of psychology at Stanford University and a lead researcher in the field of motivation.[1]

Through her research, Dr. Dweck discovered two opposing mindsets that shape the way we interact with the world. Those of us with a fixed mindset believe our character, skills, intelligence, and creative abilities remain fixed. We can do very little to improve them. People with a growth mindset believe the qualities and abilities we receive at birth represent the starting point from which we develop and grow.[2]

Dr. Dweck's work brought our public grading system under scrutiny because it operates with a fixed mindset mentality. We typically compare student achievement to either a perfect outcome or to the results of their peers. Grades deliver a final judgment because we don't offer many opportunities for students to learn and grow from their mistakes. When I failed that accounting exam, I believed my only option was to change majors. This grading system has been in place for almost ninety years, so most of us have been culturally conditioned to operate with a fixed mindset.

Thankfully, we don't have to stay there. We can adopt God's plan for us to have a growth mindset where every experience becomes an opportunity to learn and grow. One verse in the book of Proverbs illustrates God's growth mindset beautifully:

"For though the righteous fall seven times, they rise again, but the wicked stumble when calamity strikes." Proverbs 24:16

In English, we define calamity as a great misfortune or disaster. We often link it to unavoidable natural tragedies like floods or hurricanes. But the Hebrew word translated as calamity, *raah*, can mean evil, misery, distress, or injury. Because of the painful losses they cause, this Proverb can also apply to failures.

When we look at it through the lens of failure, we see God expects everyone to fail. What sets the righteous apart from the wicked is the willingness to rise again. The word seven in the scriptures often symbolizes completeness or maturity. God plans to mature us by calling us to rise up after each fall, or failure.

We see this principle played out in the lives of our Biblical heroes. The scriptures never sugarcoat the failings of its main characters. From the Old Testament to the New, the Bible weaves a story of broken people redeemed by a loving God. These men and women failed in different ways, but they had one thing in common. They all rose up from their failures and tried again. No matter how hard we try, there are times we will fall. It may be the result of our own sinful choices or because we lacked knowledge or ability. Living righteously includes learning and growing from our failures.

To help us understand how we can learn and grow from failure, let's look at the life of one of Jesus' followers.

One Disciple's Journey Through Failure

John Mark (often called Mark) is not one of the more well-known characters in the Bible. In fact, I have only heard a few lessons about him. But each time I felt drawn to him because of the failure embedded in his story.

The book of Acts gives us some insight into his life. Soon after Peter's miraculous escape from prison, John Mark joined the missionary efforts of Paul and Barnabas (Acts 12:25). For some undisclosed reason, John Mark abruptly left them and returned to Jerusalem (Acts 13:13). His departure caused a dispute to break out between Paul and Barnabas when they decided to embark on their second missionary trip:

> "Barnabas wanted to take John, also called Mark, with them, but Paul did not think it wise to take him, because he had deserted them in Pamphylia and had not continued with them in the work. They had such a sharp disagreement that they parted company. Barnabas took Mark and sailed for Cyprus, but Paul chose Silas and left, commended by the believers to the grace of the Lord. He went through Syria and Cilicia, strengthening the churches." Acts 15:37–41

Every lesson I heard about John Mark focused on this dispute. Some believe Paul should have extended grace and taken John Mark with them. Others feel Paul was justified in his decision because the dangers of missionary work required someone who is steadfast and trustworthy.

But when we focus on the dispute, we miss the bigger picture. What did John Mark learn from his failure to remain faithful to the mission work?

The hard lesson was that failure does incur loss. He lost the respect of Paul, and undoubtedly other members of the mission team. He also lost personally. The rapport he developed with Paul would have been lost. We can assume his failure caused a rift in their personal relationship. In addition to these losses, John Mark lost a valuable opportunity—to travel with Paul on his second mission trip. These losses must have hurt deeply.

But he also learned the importance of rising up after his fall. His willingness to try again taught him the redemptive side of failure. Although he lost one opportunity, he didn't lose them all. God kept a door open through Barnabas. On the surface the dispute caused division. But the Holy Spirit used the situation to double the mission work by sending out two teams instead of one.

Subsequent references in the New Testament show us that John Mark continued operating with a growth mindset. Paul listed him as a fellow worker (Philemon 1:24) and noted he had been helpful in the ministry (2 Timothy 4:11). The Holy Spirit led John Mark to write the gospel that bears his name (the Gospel of Mark). More than two thousand years later, his Gospel continues to spread the good news of Jesus.

I pray his story encourages you the way it has me. Like him, we will incur loss from failure. But if we are willing to operate with a growth mindset, we will experience the redemptive side of failure. Instead of fearing it, we can learn to appreciate its upside.

The Upside of Failure

Does the idea of favoring, or appreciating, failure seem inconceivable to you? There are so many lessons failure can teach us. Here are just a few:

Effectiveness: When we fail, we immediately gain crucial information: we know what doesn't work. A tweak on a familiar saying expresses this best: "If at first you don't succeed, figure out why. Then try again."

Perseverance: A common characteristic of successful people is perseverance. None of us learn a new skill in just one try. Those who give up too easily forfeit the success that could have been theirs.

Humility: Failure humbles us because we're forced to face our imperfections and inadequacies. This humility makes us teachable and willing to learn from surprising sources.

During my teaching days, I realized I both loved technology and hated technology. I didn't grow up with cell phones, tablets, and the Internet, so I had to painstakingly learn how to use these marvels. My young students, on the other hand, grew up speaking technology like a second language. So many times, I stood in front of my classroom SMART board and felt dumb because I couldn't get it to do what I wanted. I learned to laugh and lean into the expertise of eight-year-olds who instinctively knew what to do.

Relatability: Unless we never undertake to learn or try something new, we will fail at something. Stories of our successes may create inspiration, but nothing connects us in our humanity like the stories of our failures. Sharing them creates a vulnerability that pushes through superficiality and forges deeper relationships.

At this point you may think that learning from failure sounds great—*but how do we do it?* Let's look at how we can face our failures with a growth mindset.

Facing Failure with a Growth Mindset

When we experience failure, we feel a variety of overwhelming emotions such as shame, guilt, disappointment, embarrassment, or insecurity. To properly process failure, we need to pull away from the distractions of life and make time to sit and listen to the Holy Spirit. The amount of time we need will vary according to our emotional needs.

We begin by assuming a listening posture. Physically this means sitting with our backs straight, our feet flat on the floor, and our hands open on our laps. Spiritually this means assuming a position of humility. We know we don't have the answers, and we recognize that God does. We can set our minds by using the following sentence as a breath prayer: "Speak, Lord (inhaling), for I am listening (exhaling)."

Next, we begin to acknowledge the loss. Any failure causes us to lose something. What specifically have we lost in this failure? What is the pain associated with our loss? Then we need to give ourselves time to grieve. We can lean into God and ask Him for healing.

Once we've acknowledged and grieved our losses, we are ready to ask the following questions:

- **What is God trying to teach me through this failure?** Lessons are often multi-dimensional. They can show where we need to grow in our professional, personal, and spiritual lives.

- **What one thing could I have done differently that would have changed the outcome?** It's easy for us to want to fix everything. But let's try to focus on the one (or at the most two) areas that will create the most impact as we move forward. As the saying goes, "if everything is important, nothing is important."

- **Are there things I could do to restore what I've lost?** Sometimes we can salvage part, or all, of what we've lost. But when we can't recover our losses, we can still trust that God will work all things out for the good of those who love Him (Romans 8:28).

- **What are my next steps?** Sometimes we need to simply tweak something and keep moving forward. Other times we need to release our project, task, or situation to the Lord. Lean into the Spirit and ask for discernment to know the difference.

- **What might hold me back from rising up from this failure?** Even after processing the failure, we may feel hesitant to rise up and try again. We can ask the Spirit to infuse us with His power, love, and self-discipline so we can grow from this experience.

When we let go of our stronghold of avoiding failure, we are ready to adopt a new Spirit-led conviction: *I will favor failure as an essential part of the learning process.* And the grip performancism has on us begins to relax.

Something beautiful happens when we learn to respond to failure with a growth mindset: We rekindle the natural resilience we had as a child. We not only learn to walk, but to skip, jump, and even dance.

Pressing on Toward the Goal

Embracing the positives of failure can be so challenging. To help you with this process, sit with the Holy Spirit and reflect on the following questions:

- What is my gut reaction to the idea of failing?

- What has shaped these feelings toward failure?

- How can God's perspective help me?

Take some time to research additional scriptures on facing failure. Write out the ones that resonate with you the most. To get you started, here are a few of my favorites:

- "Not that I have already obtained all this, or have already arrived at my goal, but I press on to take hold of that for which Christ Jesus took hold of me. Brothers and sisters, I do not consider myself yet to have taken hold of it. But one thing I do: Forgetting what is behind and straining toward what is ahead, I press on toward the goal to win the prize for which God has called me heavenward in Christ Jesus." Philippians 3:12–14

- "Let us not become weary in doing good, for at the proper time we will reap a harvest if we do not give up." Galatians 6:9

- "Consider it pure joy, my brothers and sisters, whenever you face trials of many kinds, because you know that the testing of your faith produces perseverance. Let perseverance finish its work so that you may be mature and complete, not lacking anything." James 1:2–4

CHAPTER 4

Sifting

Success

"You must have accurate and honest weights and measures, so that you may live long in the land the LORD your God is giving you." Deuteronomy 25:15

My heart pounding, I opened the email from my principal. The results from the state's standardized tests had come in. Beginning in grade three, the state required students to take a series of tests to assess their grasp of grade-level content. Students' scores in each subject matter ranked their understanding as *minimal, partial, proficient*, or *advanced*.

To promote transparency, our principal grouped students' rankings by teacher and sent them out in a school-wide email. This raw data paraded before our eyes in a series of bar graphs. The percentage of our students who ranked as proficient or advanced determined our status as an effective (or ineffective) teacher.

In the aftermath of the email, the teachers divided into two groups. The ones whose students scored well walked the hallways with heads held high, exchanging nods with the other effective teachers. These teachers gathered in public places and openly congratulated each other. But the teachers whose students did not perform well slunk through the hallways with downcast eyes. They gathered in corners or private classrooms and whispered conciliatory remarks, trying to assuage the shame.

In that particular year, my students did not fare well. They had shown progress, but their performance didn't place them in the proficient or advanced categories. Their failure became mine.

Considering these test results, I emailed my principal and asked her to remove me from a future training meant for mentors of teachers. I clearly had nothing to offer the other, more proficient teachers. Even though I publicly acknowledged my epic failure, something deep inside me cried out against the unfairness of it all.

How We Measure Success Matters

In the last chapter, we explored our fear of failure and our determination to avoid it at all costs. Because failure is defined as a lack of success,[1] the need to succeed becomes a driving force in our lives. But how we measure it gets tricky. A dictionary defines success as a desired outcome, or the accomplishment of goals.[2]

All around us, we see examples of this results-oriented interpretation of achievement. We consider movies a hit or a flop based on box office sales. Successful books make various "Best Seller" lists. Public figures gauge it by the number of followers, downloads, shares, and retweets.

When we adopt this definition and use it to measure our success, we believe this lie from Satan: *Only the end result matters.* And we build our stronghold which states: *I will be successful by focusing solely on my goal.*

As self-driven achievers, we've learned to keep our eyes focused on the desired outcome and to always give our best effort. When our results don't measure up to our definition of success, we accept defeat. Yet somewhere deep inside we feel a sense of betrayal. Something just doesn't feel right or fair. Intuitively we know the end result doesn't paint the whole picture.

Until that pivotal year when my students did not perform as well as I had hoped, I never challenged measuring success only by results. But suddenly it felt unfair to judge my success solely by the performance of seven-and-eight-year-olds who had minds and wills of their own. My frustration pushed me to seek God's views on success and how we measure it. It may surprise you, as it did me, to know God has a lot to say about the types of measures we use.

One of my favorite passages on the subject of fair measurement comes from the book of Deuteronomy:

> "Do not have two differing weights in your bag—one heavy, one light. Do not have two differing measures in your house—one large, one small. You must have accurate and honest weights and measures, so that you may live long in the land the Lord your God is giving you. For the Lord your God detests anyone who does these things, anyone who deals dishonestly." Deuteronomy 25:13–16

This passage refers to a time when people used silver to purchase and sell products. To determine the silver's value, they used a balanced scale. Likewise, certain products, like grain, were sold in regulated quantities. To determine the amount of product to be sold, merchants used standardized measures (think of our use of measuring cups but on a larger scale).

Unfortunately, unscrupulous merchants found ways to give themselves an unfair advantage. These merchants used two sets of weights (one light and one heavy) and two sets of measures (one small and one large). Depending on which set they used, they cheated their customers by selling less product for more silver. Or they cheated their suppliers by buying more product for less silver (Amos 8:4–5).

While these verses speak to specific business practices, the principle has more universal applicability. God calls us to be fair in our practices and to deal honestly with one another. This includes using accurate measures and honest weights to determine our success. Let's look at how this passage applies to how we measure it.

Focusing Solely on the End Result

Defining our success solely on the end result is an inaccurate measurement because it involves a variety of factors, many of which we can't control. When we include these in our calculations, we unfairly skew the results.

For example, in my work as a teacher, my state's Department of Education chose the standardized test I gave my students. The creators of the test determined how their scores translated into levels of proficiency. Since we only looked at the end result of the test, we didn't consider how individual students would respond to the pressures of the test. Some struggled with anxiety while others failed to give their best effort.

In the year I mentioned above, one of my students had greatly improved as a reader. To accommodate family plans, he needed to take the test before our assigned time. His new testing time conflicted with our recess. As a typical eight-year-old, he wanted to play with his friends. So, he finished the test in record time by randomly selecting answers. Instead of his score bringing up my class average, it brought it down instead.

How about you? Can you think of measurements of success that include factors beyond your control? Maybe you have to meet a monthly sales quota. But to meet this goal you depend on a favorable economy or the willingness of strangers to purchase your company's product. Or maybe customer satisfaction surveys factor heavily in your employee performance appraisal. A close friend of mine often gets penalized for dissatisfied customer reviews, even when the company's policies provoked complaints.

An incredible passage nestled in the book of Isaiah can help us question the wisdom of a results-only definition of success. God is described as the Master Gardener and His people are His vineyard. He did all the necessary work for a successful harvest. He cleared the land of stones, planted the best vines, and built a watchtower and a winepress. But instead of a good harvest, the vineyard only produced bad grapes. God looked out at His people and saw bloodshed and distress rather than righteousness and justice (Isaiah 5:1–2, 7).

In light of the failure of His vineyard, God asks the following questions:

> "Now you dwellers in Jerusalem and people of Judah,
> judge between me and my vineyard.
> What more could have been done for my vineyard
> than I have done for it?
> When I looked for good grapes,
> why did it yield only bad?" Isaiah 5:3–4

How would we answer His questions? Would we say God failed? This is what our typical standards of measuring success would lead us to believe. Yet we know God did everything possible to produce a successful harvest. But because people exercised their free will, He did not experience the success He expected.

Since we wouldn't blame failure on God in the above scenario, we need to examine how we evaluate our successes or failures. Do we blame ourselves for failure when the results might have been heavily dependent on things or people we can't control? When we only look at the end result, we have an unfair measurement of success. We need to sift success using a fair measurement *and* an honest weight

Focusing Equally on the Journey

It isn't that focusing on results is wrong. The problem lies in weighing our success *only* by the final result. When we do that, we miss out on what is equally important: *enjoying the journey toward our goal.*

A shift in perspective where we can enjoy the journey keeps us present in the process instead of constantly looking into the future. Here are some benefits of focusing on our journey:

Freedom from comparison: We live in a world where the comparison trap begins early and affects us all. Comparing ourselves to others only leads to discontentment because we ignore the differences in our situations. We match our beginnings with others' endings. We liken our hard season of life to another's easy one. We forget we didn't all start from the same place or with the same resources. Focusing on our individual journeys allows us to account for these differences when we measure our success.

Lessons learned: We take time to learn what works, what doesn't work, and what works better. These lessons make us more productive and efficient.

Character development: No one has ever experienced overnight success. Reaching goals requires taking the next small step on the journey. Focusing on each step keeps us from feeling overwhelmed and builds discipline, perseverance, and patience into our character.

People we meet: We will learn from the people we meet. They may lead the way, encourage us from the sidelines, or push us from behind.

For example, in my early work as a teacher, disgruntled parents intimidated me. I would have preferred to ignore them as I pushed toward my goal. But when I took the time to lean in and listen to their concerns, I learned from their insights. They helped me improve instruction, not only for their children but for all my students.

New perspectives: Being present in the journey keeps us open and receptive to new thoughts, ideas, or actions. All of these work together to give us new perspectives on ourselves and the world around us.

The year my students didn't perform well on the state exam, and I accepted the label of ineffective teacher, my principal responded to my email with a new perspective. She pointed out the number of students in my class who spoke English as a second language. Several also struggled with emotional instabilities caused by personal trauma. Given their obstacles, they couldn't be expected to achieve at typical levels. This new perspective encouraged me to attend the mentorship training.

Once we understand the importance of giving equal weight to both the journey and the end result in the measurement of our success, we are well on our way toward destroying the stronghold we built around it. But we need to look at one more key question: *Who determines how we measure success?*

Who Determines Our Measurement?

Recently I ran across this quote: "As you climb the ladder of success, be sure it's leaning against the right building.[3]" These words express an undeniable truth. None of us wants to achieve success only to discover we pursued the wrong goal.

As we've seen, the world will always set standards and pass judgment on how well we measure against them. We can neither control nor avoid their judgments. Sometimes we have to submit to them in the workplace. But we don't have to be defined by them. We have another choice. We can learn to create our definition of success.

As I look back on that year when my students did not perform at acceptable levels, I remember the goals I had set for myself. I wanted to inspire my students with my own love for reading and learning. By ensuring they felt safe to take risks and make mistakes, I hoped to foster a growth mindset. Both of these goals aligned with the wisdom I see in God's Word.

These goals, unlike test results, couldn't be measured easily or quickly. However if successful, these objectives would continue to impact my students even after they graduate from my classroom. Employee appraisals, feedback from parents, and the rapport I enjoyed with my students told me I successfully met these goals.

While we want to respect the expectations imposed in our workplace, we can also set our own goals and align them with our priorities. How well we meet these personal goals should also factor into our overall measurement of success.

How about you? As you consider your priorities, what goals can you set for yourself? What will you use to measure your success? Are you considering God's Word in your definition?

Maybe one of your top priorities is to be a good parent. How do you define what that means? Would you only look at your children's performance in school or sports? Or would you look at their overall happiness? What does God say about parenting?

Or maybe you desire to strike a healthy work-life balance. Would you limit the overtime you work? Establish other boundaries? How would you measure your success? Are there any scriptures to use as guidelines?

It takes time and effort to both set goals that align with God's priorities and to define how we will measure our success. We also must accept that other people may not see our success in the way we do.

My principal never shared her perspective on my students' performance with the rest of the staff. In the eyes of some of my colleagues, I still bore the label of an ineffective teacher. I had to make peace with knowing the truth. Since we used inaccurate measures and dishonest weights to determine success, some of my colleague's successes, like my failure, had been overstated.

When we learn, as self-driven achievers, to use God's measure of success, we will walk in freedom. We will no longer sift our success through the lenses of the world but through our own set of weights and measures. And we don't have to do this alone. Let's look at how the Holy Spirit can help us create our definition of success.

Defining Success with a Spiritual Mindset

Self-driven achievers find it easy to set goals. Carefully defining our success, however, does not come naturally. Too often we settle on the final result because it's easy to see and to measure. But we know it doesn't tell the whole story. To help us properly define what success will mean, we need to create time and space to understand the big picture.

As we think about it, we need to remember our ultimate goal is to lead successful lives. Any definition of success must consider how this will look in all facets of our lives, professional, personal, and spiritual.

To help us with this process, we can take time to visualize how we want our lives to look at the end of the next month, quarter, or year. Where do we hope to be professionally? Are we planning a career move, looking for a promotion, or seeking more training? What changes do we hope to see in our overall health? Do we need to make room for more rest, exercise, or meal planning? What kind of person do we want to be? In what areas do we want to become more like Christ? What balance do we want to see in our professional, personal, and spiritual lives?

Each aspect of our lives impacts the others. For example, if we set a personal goal to spend more time with our family, we may have to reduce the hours we work. If we set a spiritual goal to be more active in our church community, we may need to cut back on some other pastimes. Once we have a vision for the big picture of our lives, we are ready to set goals and define our measurements of success.

Think about one of your current goals—be it spiritual, professional, or personal. To begin the process, pull away from the distractions of life and ask the Spirit for discernment as you seek answers to questions like the following:

- What end result do I hope to attain?

- Where do I need to sift success?

- How much will I need to rely on other people and situations to help me achieve my goal?

- How much time will I need?

- Are there Biblical principles that I can apply?

- Can I meditate on specific scriptures to help me stay motivated?

- What do I hope to learn or discover as I journey toward the end goal? How can the journey help me grow in my character?

As you reflect on the answers to these questions, tweak your goal, or add a second one, so that your measurement of success will be fair and honest—not solely dependent on people and situations you can't control.

At different intervals in your journey, take time to pull away and reflect:

- How has the process been so far?

- What have I learned or discovered?

- What am I thankful for?

- What has been challenging?

- What successes have I seen to date?

- How well am I progressing toward my goals?

- Do I need to tweak my goals in any way?

- Do I need more time?

- In what ways am I tempted to follow the results-oriented mindset of the world?

- Where do I need to lean on the power, love, and self-discipline of the Holy Spirit?

Once you have reflected and found answers to these questions, you will know how to move forward.

Relying on the wisdom of the Holy Spirit to set goals may be a new experience. It may even feel awkward and time-consuming. But if we persevere, we will discover how to balance the final outcome with the journey. As we let go of our stronghold of only considering the results, we are ready to adopt our new Spirit-led conviction: *I will sift my success by using fair and accurate measurements. The progress toward my goal is just as valuable as the end result.*

When we let God help us define and measure our success, our peace and joy can't be shaken—even when others don't recognize what we accomplished. We will be one step closer to loosening the grip of performancism and embracing the Spirit-led life.

Pressing on Toward the Goal

As you process the content in this chapter, sit with the Holy Spirit and reflect on the following questions:

- How have I measured success in the past?

- What can I gain by focusing not only on the desired end result but also on the journey toward that goal?

- In what ways do I struggle with the comparison trap and letting the world define my success or failure?

- Which of the benefits of the journey do I see as most helpful?

Research additional scriptures on godly success. Write out the ones that resonate with you the most. Here are a few of my favorites:

- "For I know the plans I have for you,' declares the LORD, 'plans to prosper you and not to harm you, plans to give you hope and a future." Jeremiah 29:11

- "Blessed is the one who does not walk in step with the wicked or stand in the way that sinners take or sit in the company of mockers, but whose delight is in the law of the LORD, and who meditates on his law day and night. That person is like a tree planted by streams of water, which yields its fruit in season and whose leaf does not wither—whatever they do prospers." Psalm 1:1–3

- "For this very reason, make every effort to add to your faith goodness; and to goodness, knowledge; and to knowledge, self-control; and to self-control, persever-ance; and to perseverance, godliness; and to godliness, mutual affection; and to mutual affection, love. For if you possess these qualities in increasing measure, they will keep you from being ineffective and unproductive in your knowledge of our Lord Jesus Christ." 2 Peter 1:5–8

CHAPTER 5

Aligning Allegiance

"Fear of man will prove to be a snare,
but whoever trusts in the Lord is kept safe."
Proverbs 29:25

The deafening silence blanketing his office threatened to suffocate me. With my heart pounding in my ears, I recognized the papers spread out on his massive desk.

That morning the managing partner of the CPA firm had called me in for my exit interview. On my resignation form, I listed excessive overtime as my reason for quitting.

As he pointed to my timesheets, a flush crept up my neck and face. He repeated his question. "Can you explain why these timesheets do not reflect this excessive overtime you claim?"

Unable to speak, I lifted my eyes to his. We both knew the answer. But neither of us wanted to accept its consequences. So, we continued to ignore the elephant in the room.

I had committed the crime of eating time, meaning I didn't record hours worked over the budget; I "ate" them.

Professionals bill their clients for services rendered. At the accounting firm, we all kept meticulous records of our time in fifteen-minute intervals. Compilations of these time logs generated client invoices. Simply put, the more hours spent on a client, the more money earned. But there was a caveat.

Before engaging a client, the firm submitted a budget. To justify budget overages, we needed to prove the client responsible. For example, a client's indecipherable financial records or uncooperative employees could cause us to work extra hours. But no client would agree to pay for additional time needed due to the accountant's inexperience or inefficiency.

Officially, the firm discouraged eating time. Unofficially it became our unspoken practice. Since we worked on jobs in teams, if one person went over budget, it meant we all went over budget. All of our evaluations, from staff accountant to manager, depended on how well we performed at or under budget. Everyone felt the pressure.

At first, I downplayed it. "I need to deduct a few minutes for going to the restroom, taking a break to get a soda, or time spent on the phone." Then I justified it. "I'm doing this for everyone else. I don't want them to get a poor evaluation because of me."

But the real reason I lied on those timesheets? I didn't want to disappoint my colleagues by failing to complete my work within the budgeted time.

So the two of us sat, frozen in stony silence. I imagine my nonverbal confession unleashed a flurry of unanswered questions. My boss surely wondered if I was the only one eating time. (I wasn't).

How many undocumented and unbilled hours existed in the firm? Hours that potentially equated to thousands of lost revenue dollars. Revenue which would have translated into increased personal income for him.

And me? I realized I had failed in the most miserable way. Holding myself out as a Christian, I often talked about my faith in Jesus. Some of my coworkers had visited my church. Yet here I sat, a *liar*. Not only had I destroyed my credibility, but I also tainted the image of the One I followed.

Finally, and without another word, the partner sighed, signed my form, and dismissed me. As I slinked out the door, I vowed to never again violate my conscience by giving in to peer pressure.

The Pressure to Please

The phrase people-pleaser typically describes people who willingly disregard their own needs and interests to obtain the approval or acceptance of others. While healthy forms exist, such as negotiation and compromise, we usually associate people-pleasing with negative connotations.

All around us, we see evidence that success is tied to popularity. Popular athletes, entertainment personalities, or social media influencers often receive lucrative financial endorsements, rewards, and perks. So we easily fall for this lie from Satan: *My ability to be successful depends on my popularity.* And we build a stronghold that states: *I will do whatever is necessary so people will like and accept me.* This stronghold keeps us tied to perfomancism and hinders us from a Spirit-led life.

Subconsciously we know our desire to please others does not come from a healthy place. At its core, people-pleasing forces us to align ourselves with the agendas and expectations of others—sometimes with disastrous results. Avoiding disapproval or rejection in our relationships can cause us to fail in other important areas of our lives. God warns us of this in the book of Proverbs:

> "Fear of man will prove to be a snare, but whoever trusts in the LORD is kept safe." Proverbs 29:25

The deep roots to please others often propel us to unwanted behaviors that yield unwelcomed results. My fear of disappointing others led me to violate company policy. Even worse, my desire to please caused me to compromise what was most important to me, my faith.

People-pleasing can be seen played out in a variety of similar scenarios:

- Receptionists and secretaries who lied so others could dodge a phone call.

- Pastors who fudged their attendance and membership records so their church would appear healthy and vibrant.

- Teachers who gave in to parental and administrative pressure by giving students a grade they didn't earn.

- Women who engaged in sexual activity before they felt ready to avoid losing a relationship.

- Teens who followed the crowd into alcohol or drug use, or other illegal activities, to be seen as "cool."

- People who pursued someone else's dreams and goals while suppressing their own.

Admittedly, the consequences of some of these situations are more damaging than others. But when we repeatedly silence our true beliefs, feelings, goals, and dreams, we begin losing our authenticity. Over time this gives way to anger, resentment, bitterness, and deep regret. It can also lead to physical ailments such as addictions and eating disorders.

As a self-driven achiever, can you think of times now, or in the past, when your people-pleasing desires caused you to act in a certain way to win the approval or acceptance of others? To avoid the snares of these tendencies, we first need to understand the connection between success and popularity. Research does reveal a link, but not in the way we think.

Two Types of Popularity Influence Our People-Pleasing Ways

Dr. Mitch Prinstein Ph.D., a psychology professor at the University of North Carolina at Chapel Hill and author of *Popular*, spent twenty years researching popularity.[1] His research led him to identify two types.

The first, status popularity, reflects our *social reputation*. This is what we normally think of when we think of popularity. The more others see us as influential, visible, powerful, and dominant, the more admired we become. When we have this type, we achieve a certain social status.

Part of the persona of the self-driven achiever is the desire to project the image of "having it all together." Social status ranks high in our priorities. So we work hard to perfect and protect our masks of competence which serve to hide our inadequacies.

To validate my social reputation, I feel driven to pursue the next promotion or to be seen with the right people or at the right places. How about you? Do you find yourself craving recognition for your accomplishments? This desire can push us to align our allegiance in the wrong ways, trying to please people whose approval and acceptance will advance our social reputation.

In today's world, social media has taken this pursuit to a whole new level. Facebook, Instagram, and X (formally Twitter) count the number of friends, likes, shares, and reposts, making it easy for us to calculate and then compare our level of status popularity. Have you known people who keep running tabs of the number of likes on their Facebook posts so they can compare it to those of their friends? How do you feel when your posts receive a lot of traffic? How do you feel when they don't?

The second type of popularity, called likability, reflects *social preference.*[2] The more others see us as likable, the more they will prefer us. To some extent, we all want to be liked. The way we define *likable* drives our people-pleasing ways.

What attributes come to mind when you think of being likable? How does the presence of conflict affect your definition of likability? Many of us perceive conflict as a threat to our ability to be liked. So to keep peace, we surrender our agendas, opinions, and even our principles.

However, in his research, Dr. Prinstein found social preference doesn't mean an absence of conflict. Contrary to what we may believe, true likability comes from cultivating attributes with universal appeal such as making everyone feel heard, important, valued, and included.[3] The more we express empathy, kindness, and the willingness to listen, the more likable, or preferable, we become to others.

Of the two types of popularity, Dr. Prinstein advises us to pursue likability.[4] According to his research, status popularity may bring temporary successful results, but it does little to build long-term happiness. Likability, on the other hand, predicts longer lives, better health, and stronger relationships at both work and home.

It's a relief to know likability doesn't depend on the approval of others but on our ability to value others by making them feel important. However, becoming more likable doesn't mean *everyone will like us*. It's a question of allegiance. Let's look at how Jesus modeled this for us.

Likable vs. Liked—A Question of Allegiance

In His teaching on the two greatest commandments, Jesus defined the order of our allegiance: first to God, and second to people:

> "Jesus replied: 'Love the Lord your God with all your heart and with all your soul and with all your mind.' This is the first and greatest commandment. And the second is like it: 'Love your neighbor as yourself.'"
>
> Matthew 22:37–39

Jesus modeled these commandments during His time on earth. His first priority was always to please His Father (John 8:29). Throughout His ministry, Jesus also loved people. But this didn't mean Jesus granted their every request. He loved people by meeting their most important need—restoring their relationship with God.

In the process, Jesus displayed the traits of likability. He consistently engaged with people who lived on the margins of His society. The gospel writers include many accounts of Jesus socializing with sinners and tax collectors. He extended compassion to people suffering from diseases, especially leprosy.

Jesus also respected women and children, two groups of people who were considered unimportant by His culture.

Despite being likable, not everyone liked, accepted, or approved of Jesus. Conflict arose from His allegiance to His Father and His inclusion of "undesirable" people. We see this most often with the religious leaders, but disputes also happened with His family and friends. Toward the end of His ministry, a large number of His followers began to turn away. At one time scholars believe Jesus had 15,000 to 20,000 followers,[5] but only a few stayed with Him at the crucifixion. Most notably these were His mother, some of the other women, and the apostle John (John 19:25–27). After His resurrection, the believers numbered only about 120 (Acts 1:15).

In the gospel accounts, people usually fell "out of like" with Jesus for one of the following reasons:

- He didn't meet their preconceived expectations.

- He challenged them to seek spiritual, rather than physical, blessings.

- His teachings were too hard to accept or to follow.

- His plan seemed too scary or dangerous.

In other words, people left Jesus because they didn't like, accept, or approve of His agenda and plan. Jesus could stand with confidence against the dislike of people because He cared more about pleasing His Father and fulfilling His purpose.

While Jesus does teach us how to be more likable, He also shows us that *being liked* depends on how well others appreciate God's agenda and expectations. Accepting this truth can help us change our people-pleasing ways.

Escaping the Snare of People-Pleasing

After leaving the accounting firm, I accepted a supervisory position on the audit team of a prominent bank. I refused to compromise my faith, but I also made it a point to be approachable and supportive to the members of my team. My efforts seemed to pay off when I was invited to join an elite leadership training program.

This training was extremely challenging, and I began to flounder with one of my assignments. I reached out to one of my favorite managers for help. Doubting I would meet the deadline for my assignment, he abruptly switched course.

"Shirley," he interjected, "people like *you* need people like *me* to explain the way the world works."

Immediately I felt uneasy. Can anything good come from wanting to teach the ways of the world to a follower of Jesus?

"Here's what you do," he continued. "Place a few sheets of paper in an unsealed envelope and take it down to our mailroom. Tell the postal worker you are waiting for some papers to be completed, but you need the envelope postmarked today. They will leave the envelope unsealed. Take all the time you need for the assignment and send it in when you're done."

Almost of its own volition, my head began to shake, "No." Immediately enraged, his demeanor changed.

"Why are you saying no? It's not wrong, it's not a sin," he spat out. "Everyone does this! I've done it, and so has…" He rattled off all the managers of our division and threw in our director's name for good measure.

"It's lying." The sound of my voice, clear and calm, astounded me.

"It's not lying," he countered. "It's normal business practice."

We sat at a standstill for a few moments. Finally, I thanked him for his time and left his office. We both knew I would not give myself extra time on the assignment by being deceitful with the postmark.

Up until this confrontation, my manager and I enjoyed a friendly, professional relationship. I wish I could say we moved past this situation and regained our easy footing. But we never did. For the rest of my time with the company, our relationship remained tense and strained.

When I think of the lost relationship, I still feel sad. But the memory doesn't invoke regret or shame. In their place stands the peace gained from aligning my allegiance to the Lord and not the world. We can break free from the snare of people-pleasing. But first, we need to recognize our temptation. Then we need to set our hearts on pleasing God.

Recognizing the Temptation to Please People

Sometimes we readily recognize the temptation to please people, as when my manager suggested being deceitful with the postmark. Other times the desire to please people is more subtle because it is mixed with pure motives. Wanting to earn the respect of my coworkers so I could share the Gospel with them led me to lie on my timesheets at the accounting firm. I didn't recognize the snares of my people-pleasing ways until my managing partner confronted them.

Like me, you may find it difficult to immediately recognize when you are falling into people-pleasing behaviors. Here are a couple of practices we can adopt to help us:

Learn the people-pleasing "tells." There are certain emotions or mannerisms that signal we are heading into people-pleasing territory. One big tell is a nagging feeling that we're violating our conscience. This leads to mental gymnastics as we try to downplay or justify our actions.

For me, another big tell is a general sense of uneasiness, especially when I face unfamiliar situations or meet new people. This discomfort pushes me to say things I don't necessarily mean, all to impress. There are also times when I feel prompted by the Holy Spirit to share my point of view. But when I'm afraid of upsetting others, I feel tempted to either hold back or say what I think they want to hear.

Process the "tells" with the help of the Holy Spirit. When we catch ourselves falling into people-pleasing mode, we can pull away from all distractions and sit with the Holy Spirit. As we assume a listening stance, we can ask the Spirit to help us discern what is prompting this desire to please people. We can ask questions like: Where am I violating my conscience? What do I think I'll gain by giving in to the pressure to please others? What do I stand to lose? Do I need reminders of my worth to God, so I don't seek it in the acceptance of these people? What would Jesus do in my situation?

Knowing our tells and processing them with the Holy Spirit helps us to first identify and then renounce our tendencies. This sets our hearts free to please God.

Setting Our Hearts on Pleasing God

Setting our hearts on pleasing God won't always make us popular. Sometimes, as with my manager, our decisions will challenge people who don't embrace God's standards of holiness. Jesus warned us that some people will prefer the darkness because they don't want to expose their evil deeds (John 3:19–20). These people will fall "out of like" with us, not because we are unlikable, but because we imitate Jesus. And although it may hurt when someone dislikes us, disapproves of us, or no longer accepts us, we will maintain our integrity and experience His peace.

Other times our allegiance to God may cause us to make some unpopular, life-altering decisions. Over thirty years ago, I chose to move to Paris, France and serve a small mission church. This decision did not please all the people in my life at the time. But when we faithfully follow God's path for us, we can confidently accept the disapproval of others.

Experiencing opposition from people is never easy. To help us stand against the pushback of others, we can meditate on specific scriptures. Our key verse for this chapter can be one of our main inspirations:

> "Fear of man will prove to be a snare, but whoever trusts
> in the LORD is kept safe." Proverbs 29:25

We can also visualize scenes from the Bible. For example, in the book of Acts, Luke describes Stephen, the first martyr for Jesus. If you are unfamiliar with his story, you can find it in Acts 7. Let's look at a few key points.

Stephen was martyred because his preaching for Jesus brought him into opposition with some of the Jewish leaders. Just before he was stoned to death, Stephen looked up to heaven and saw Jesus *standing at the right hand of God* (Acts 7:55–56). The New Testament records many instances where Jesus is *at* God's right hand, but this is the only place where Jesus is seen standing. In the Jewish court system, witnesses stood to give their testimony.[6] Some scholars believe Jesus offered Stephen solidarity and support by standing as a witness for him.

When we stand up for Jesus and align our allegiance with Him, we don't usually suffer the same intense opposition as Stephen. But when we face the possibility of losing a relationship or incurring repercussions in the workplace, this image of Jesus can comfort us. Knowing He both sees and approves of our choices to please God, rather than people, can give us strength.

Because Jesus set His heart on pleasing God, He successfully fulfilled His mission and purpose. His life proves that popularity does not equal success. Accepting this truth frees us to let go of our people-pleasing stronghold which ties us to performancism. In its place we can adopt a new, Spirit-led conviction: *I will align myself with Jesus. People will respond to me in the same ways as they did to Him.*

As we move forward with a Spirit-led life, not everyone will cheer for us and our choices. But when we stand for Jesus, He will stand for us.

Pressing on Toward the Goal

It's easy to fall into the trap of pleasing people. To understand how this desire manifests in your life, remove yourself from all distractions and sit with the Holy Spirit. Ask Him to help you answer the following questions:

- Where do I struggle to please people in order to establish or maintain my social status?

- How would it look for me to pursue being likable instead of being liked? How would this change the way I interact with the people in my life?

- When have I compromised my convictions or integrity to please other people? What did I gain? What did I lose? How do I feel about that experience?

- What are my "tells"—the emotions or mannerisms that signal I am heading into people-pleasing mode?

Take some time to research additional scriptures on living to please God rather than people. Write out the ones that resonate with you the most. To get you started, here are a few of my favorites:

- "This is the verdict: Light has come into the world, but people loved darkness instead of light because their deeds were evil. Everyone who does evil hates the light, and will not come into the light for fear that their deeds will be exposed. But whoever lives by the truth comes into the light, so that it may be seen plainly that what they have done has been done in the sight of God." John 3:19–21

- "If the world hates you, keep in mind that it hated me first. If you belonged to the world, it would love you as its own. As it is, you do not belong to the world, but I have chosen you out of the world. That is why the world hates you. Remember what I told you: 'A servant is not greater than his master.' If they persecuted me, they will persecute you also. If they obeyed my teaching, they will obey yours also. They will treat you this way because of my name, for they do not know the one who sent me." John 15:18–21

- "When the LORD takes pleasure in anyone's way, he causes their enemies to make peace with them." Proverbs 16:7

CHAPTER 6

Building

Boundaries

"In vain you rise early
and stay up late,
toiling for food to eat—
for he grants sleep to those he loves."
Psalm 127:2

Mystified, I took the folded magazine clipping from my sister-in-law. I opened it and read these words:

> "The only thing more overrated than natural child-birth is the joy of owning your own business."

Catching her eyes, we both collapsed with laughter. A few months earlier I had started my own accounting practice. Becoming my own boss had ushered into my life a whole new set of challenges. The words on the paper she handed me resonated with truth.

I don't see the words on the clipping as discounting either natural childbirth or owning your own business. The key lies in the word "overrated." In our zeal to praise the benefits of anything, we tend to gloss over its downsides. This certainly held true for me as I joyfully became self-employed.

I began my accounting practice when I was pregnant with my second child. Without hesitation, I bought into the hype of being my boss. I wanted to work from home and still be a stay-at-home mom. I imagined choosing my hours and working as much, or as little, as I wanted. Rather than submitting to someone else's priorities, I looked forward to running my practice according to my work ethic and philosophy.

However, building my practice took time. I started with very few clients which left many of my workdays open. Taking advantage of this newfound freedom, I began to say "yes" to all the opportunities I had to decline when I worked full-time. I began volunteering in my daughter's classroom and accepted a position on the governing board of a nonprofit organization. Soon I found myself participating in various ministries of my home church.

At first, owning my business seemed idyllic. I had finally achieved balance in my life. But my family began to feel the impact of losing the steady income from my former job. So to compensate, I took on every client who approached me. Sometimes the work fell outside of the normal accounting and tax services I offered. As my practice grew, so did my busyness. And my life started to spiral out of control.

The Struggle to Say "No"

As self-driven achievers, we find it difficult, if not impossible, to say "no" to the invitations, requests, or demands that come our way. As we overextend ourselves, we neglect our personal needs and fail to protect our health. We believe Satan's lie: *I can do it all if I just work harder.* And we build a stronghold that states: *I will ignore my personal needs and boundaries so I can serve others.*

Can you think of times when you said "yes" too readily and overextended yourself? Maybe you agreed to take on extra work for a colleague. Or you volunteered to spearhead a project even though your plate was already full. What negative consequences did you experience as a result?

After only a couple of months of running my new business, disillusionment settled in. Although some clients allowed me to work from home, many insisted I come to them. This meant I had to arrange daycare for my children.

Several of my new clients were women entrepreneurs. They decided to go into business for themselves in hopes of a better balance between work and family. I understood their priorities and wanted to be helpful, so I worked around their schedules. But in the process, I lost control over my own.

And all those other activities to which I had said "yes"? Since I gave my word, I honored my commitments. All those once-empty workdays in my calendar became filled with work appointments or volunteer activities.

Whenever possible, I worked from home. But I soon learned infants and toddlers don't always cooperate when Mommy has to work. More and more I found myself working into the wee hours of the morning because it was the only time no one needed me. After a few short hours of sleep, I'd get up and start the process over again.

What happened to all the benefits of running my own business? With a wink and a promise, my new boss (aka me) chased any doubts away. "You can do it all," I told myself, "you just have to work a little harder."

Whenever anyone questioned how much I worked, I laughed it off. I got through college by pulling all-night study sessions. I seemed to have the remarkable ability to burn the candle at both ends without any consequences. I read Psalm 127:2 (God grants sleep to those He loves) and quipped, "God must not love me, because I don't get sleep!"

I meant for my joke to be playful. I *knew* God loved me. After all, He sent His Son to die for me. I expressed my gratitude to Him by working so hard. As the apostle Paul taught, "Whatever you do, work at it with all your heart, as working for the Lord, not for human masters" (Colossians 3:23).

But after a few months, my grueling schedule began to wear on me. Now in my sleep-deprived state, I saw Psalm 127:2 in a different light. I began to half-believe God didn't love me.

The Slippery Slope of Sleep Deprivation

The truth noted in Psalm 127:2 cannot be ignored. It reads, "In vain you rise early and stay up late, toiling for food to eat—for he grants sleep to those he loves." Our sleep suffers when we work too hard. And when we don't get enough sleep, we open the door to a whole host of other problems.

In the short term, a lack of sleep can lead to increased moodiness, daytime drowsiness, reduced alertness, and short-term memory loss.[1] These in turn can lead to relationship problems, dependence on caffeine or other stimulants, and an increased risk of making mistakes. Long-term consequences include high blood pressure, diabetes, heart attacks, heart failure, or stroke.[2]

My lack of sleep carried more of these consequences than I willingly admitted. Family and friends always took a backseat to my work. I caught myself snapping at those I love the most. I drank way too much coffee. And I made some *big* mistakes.

On one occasion, I worked in the middle of the night on a tax return for one of my pastors. But something seemed off when I reviewed the return. After consulting tax reference materials, I decided my software program had made a mistake. I "corrected" the return and sent it off. The pastor would receive a huge refund. I was a hero!

Until a few months later when the government regulatory agency reviewed the tax return and found my error. The pastor had to repay the refund, plus interest. Since I made the mistake, I offered to refund the tax return fee and pay the penalty. My pastor treated me with amazing grace, even though my error caused him financial stress. He didn't ask me to pay anything, and he readily forgave me. But the situation left me shattered. I didn't understand how God could allow me to make such a colossal mistake when I tried so hard to honor Him in my work.

It's hard sometimes to reconcile seemingly conflicting passages like Colossians 3:23 and Psalm 127:2. But when we step back and read the first verse of Psalm 127, we gain some insightful context:

> "Unless the Lord builds the house,
>   the builders labor in vain.
>   Unless the Lord watches over the city,
>   the guards stand watch in vain."

This verse of Psalm 127 teaches us the importance of relying on God in our work, rather than ourselves. It is possible to work with all our heart and get enough sleep. The trick is to trust God and the boundaries He creates.

God's Boundaries

We create boundaries as a form of protection. In the simplest sense, boundaries keep in what is good and helpful and keep out what is bad and harmful. One of my favorite analogies is of a playground built next to a busy street. Building a fence around the playground keeps the children safe inside and away from the traffic on the outside. Within the limits of the fence, children feel free to run and play.

In the scriptures, God created boundaries for us in the form of His decrees. When we step outside of His law, we undermine His protection. We can do this in one of two ways:

Sins of commission: We engage in thoughts or behaviors that God specifically banned. For example, God warns us against participating in sexual immorality, hatred, fits of rage, jealousy, selfishness, and drunkenness (Galatians 5:19–21). When we abstain from these types of behaviors, we protect ourselves from what is bad and harmful.

Sins of omission: We fail to engage in thoughts or behaviors that God requires. Scripture continuously encourages us to do good. For example, we are called to first love the Lord with all our heart, soul, and mind, and then love our neighbor as ourselves (Matthew 22:37–39). When we obey these decrees, we protect ourselves by keeping in all that is good and helpful.

As self-driven achievers, we love rules and regulations. They become a checklist for us to complete. We excel at doing. But there are a group of commands which we tend to overlook. These decrees instruct us to stop all our activity and simply rest.

Our self-driven natures push us to ignore God's instructions to rest. Obeying all the other commandments helps us feel useful and effective. But the idea of taking time to rest feels counter-productive. So we can easily neglect a critical element of God's protective boundary. But once we open our eyes to the command to rest, we find this theme woven throughout the Old and New Testaments.

God modeled rest. Unlike us, God never tires or grows weary (Isaiah 40:28). Yet He instituted the concept of rest and modeled it for us: "Then God blessed the seventh day and made it holy, because on it he rested from all the work of creating that he had done" (Genesis 2:3).

Jesus instructed His disciples to rest. Jesus sent out His twelve apostles to preach a message of repentance (Mark 6:7–12). When they returned, they were so busy they didn't even have time to eat. So Jesus instructed them to rest, "Come with me by your-selves to a quiet place and get some rest" (Mark 6:31b).

Jesus promised rest for us. In Matthew 11:28 Jesus promised, "Come to me, all you who are weary and burdened, and I will give you rest." Originally, these words referred to the burdens the Jewish people felt from trying to follow both the written law and the oral tradition.[3] Yet the promise resonates with us because we all feel burdened and weary by the trials and tribulations of life.

In the Old Testament, the word "rest" comes from the Hebrew word, *shabath*, which means to cease or desist.[4] The Greek word for "rest" used in the New Testament, *anapauó*, means to take an intermission from labor or to refresh.[5] God intends for us to have a rhythm, or balance, of work and rest.

As self-driven achievers, we need to learn the value of getting adequate sleep (which rests our bodies) and taking breaks from our work during our waking hours (which rests our minds and spirits). God created us with the need for both kinds of rest. And it should come as no surprise, that science backs this up.

Benefits of Rest

My research on the benefits of rest surprised me. I didn't expect them to affect so many aspects of our lives. Here are a few examples of how rest boosts our physical, emotional, and professional lives:

Physical benefits: The number one benefit of rest is a reduction in cortisol, the stress hormone. Stress has been linked to heart disease, high blood pressure, and weight gain.[6] Adequate rest helps us avoid these health problems. Rest also boosts our immune system. If we use our breaks from our work to move (walk, exercise), we can actually increase our life span.[7]

Emotional benefits: Rest stabilizes our moods and emotions. Can you think of times when you experienced irritability, impatience, and emotional outbursts due to inadequate rest? Depression and anxiety are also linked to rest deprivation.[8] Building enough rest into our schedules allows us to not only enjoy healthier emotions, but it also enhances our overall satisfaction in life.

Professional benefits: Rest revives our mental energy and leads to increased creativity. It also heightens our focus and strengthens our short-term memory. All these benefits actually lead to greater productivity.[9]

Do any of these surprise you? Does the idea of rest boosting productivity seem contradictory? Often God's ways don't make sense to us. Yet my own experiences bear out this truth about rest.

For years I followed the adage, "Work first, play second." But my work never ended. You may have heard of Parkinson's Law which states, "Work expands to fill the time allotted for its completion."[10] When we don't schedule time to rest, our tasks can easily take up all our available time. This leaves very little (if any) time to rest.

Understanding God's principle of rest leads us to follow a new model: *Work, rest, work, rest.* When we schedule pockets of time for rest, we will experience God's wisdom. We will still finish our work projects. But we will also have time to invest in our relationships, as well as to pursue other personal interests and hobbies. Taking time to rest will lead to a more productive and happier life.

If I had understood this principle of rest years ago when I first entered the workforce, I could have spared myself some pain and stress. But even when we do understand His teaching on rest, we need to trust God to obey it.

As self-driven achievers we like feeling needed or important, so it's easy for us to say "yes" to every request that comes our way. But when we lack an honest estimate of our time or resources, we quickly overextend ourselves.

All of my "yeses" meant I filled my schedule with activities, many of which didn't align with my personal skill set or talents. Some of these activities brought me no joy or satisfaction. My lack of boundaries caused disharmony between the life I lived and the life I wanted. To create healthy boundaries, I needed to understand when to trust God by saying "no."

Trusting God Enough to Say "No"

God's Word provides us with the wisdom we need to confidently refuse certain demands from others. In Galatians 6, the Bible tells us to carry each other's burdens, but for everyone to carry his own load (Galatians 6:2–5). The Greek word for "load," *phortion*, refers to an individual responsibility that can't be transferred to another person.[11] On the other hand, the Greek word for "burden," *baros*, means a weight or a trouble.[12] Because burdens threaten to crush us, we need others to help us carry them. Loads, on the other hand, are meant to be our responsibility.

We may think it's easier and less time-consuming to step in and take over someone else's load. But when we teach others to meet their own responsibilities, we free ourselves of unnecessary stress and hardships.

The Bible also encourages us to let people suffer the consequences of their mistakes or bad planning. Proverbs 19:19 warns, "A hot-tempered person must pay the penalty; rescue them, and you will have to do it again." Although this verse applies specifically to rescuing angry people, the principle can apply to other situations.

When we rescue others from the results of their actions, we strip them of the ability to learn from their mistakes. This means they will continue to repeat their errors—and expect us to rescue them.

Knowing when to say "no" doesn't come naturally. It takes practice. We can start by replacing our impulsive "yes" with "Let me think about it and get back to you." Then we can press for more details: "How much time do you need from me each week/month/quarter? What resources do you need me to provide? How long of a commitment do you need—in terms of weeks, months, or years?" Finally, we can enlist the help of the Holy Spirit.

After pulling away from distractions, we can sit with the Spirit and ask for wisdom as we reflect on questions like the following: Will I be taking on someone else's load (responsibility)? Am I trying to rescue someone? Do I want to take on this responsibility, or do I feel obligated? Does this task fall within my natural wheelhouse of skills, or will I need to learn something new? Will taking on this request cause me to compromise my work/life balance or squeeze out opportunities for rest?

Often the decision to accept or decline the request becomes clear through this process. If it doesn't, we stay in a listening posture until it either becomes clear or we need to give an answer. If we haven't received a clear "yes", we can follow this rule: "When in doubt, don't."

Taking the time to process these types of requests will give us the confidence we need to say "no" when appropriate. The more we practice this process, the easier it will become. When we trust God enough to say "no," we build margins in our schedule for rest. It also frees us to say "yes" to those requests which bring us the most joy and satisfaction.

Freeing Ourselves to Say "Yes"

When we don't have to say "yes" to everything, we can freely accept those requests and opportunities for which we are best suited. The apostle Peter wrote, "Each of you should use whatever gift you have received to serve others, as faithful stewards of God's grace in its various forms" (1Peter 4:10). From his words, we know God created each of us with unique gifts. Using them for His glory will bring us joy.

To do this, we need to have a balanced and fair assessment of our gifts. Do you feel comfortable declaring your gifts? Many of us question our ability to be objective. If you struggle to identify your God-given gifts, here are some great tips:

Reflect on your childhood: Before the world began screaming ideas and expectations at us, we naturally gravitated toward the gifts He gave us. What were your favorite pastimes as a child? Did you show a natural aptitude for any particular skills?

Assess your training: After reflecting on your instinctual interests, consider any training you've received. What are some skills you've acquired through your work or personal hobbies?

Consider the opinions of others: Think back to the compliments you've received. Do they reflect a certain gift or talent? Have you been told you are gifted in certain areas?

Take a free online test: A quick Google search will uncover many websites that offer free assessments to help you pinpoint your gifts. Often these tests will uncover skills or talents you hadn't thought of before.

Adopt a holistic approach: It's easy to think some gifts are useful for the church, while others are more suitable for our careers. But the beauty of our gifts is that they enhance everything we do. We can use our secular training to serve the church, and we can use our spiritual gifts to help us shine in the workplace.

A few years ago, I agreed to serve in the children's ministry. But when I was assigned to the infant room, my heart sank. I love babies. But the teaching in that classroom consisted of singing spiritual songs. If you've ever sat next to me in church, you know I sing with joy but no talent! The infant room just wasn't the best fit for my skills and gifts.

Finally, I asked the children's ministry leader to change my assignment. Moving to an elementary class allowed me to use my training as a schoolteacher, and my joy in serving increased dramatically.

God never intended for us to do everything, or to satisfy all the needs and demands that come our way. When we learn how to decide which requests to accept, and which ones to decline, we will loosen the grip of perfomancism. In place of our self-driven stronghold, we can adopt our new Spirit-led conviction: *I will build boundaries and trust meeting this God-given need will protect my overall well-being.* As we relax the grip of performancism, we are well on our way to enjoying a Spirit-led life.

Pressing on Toward the Goal

Setting healthy boundaries is difficult for the self-driven achiever. Take some time to sit with the Holy Spirit, away from all distractions, and reflect on the following questions:

- How is my work/life balance?

- How do I feel about rest? What do my actions reveal about how I feel about rest?

- Of the many activities vying for my attention, which ones align best with my natural talents and learned skills? Which ones bring me the most joy and satisfaction?

Research additional scriptures on the wisdom of creating boundaries. Write out the ones that resonate with you the most. To get you started, here are a few of my favorites:

- "LORD, you alone are my portion and my cup; you make my lot secure. The boundary lines have fallen for me in pleasant places; surely I have a delightful inheritance." Psalm 16:5–6

- "If any of you lacks wisdom, you should ask God, who gives generously to all without finding fault, and it will be given to you." James 1:5

- "Be very careful, then, how you live—not as unwise but as wise, making the most of every opportunity, because the days are evil. Therefore do not be foolish, but understand what the Lord's will is." Ephesians 5:15–17

CHAPTER 7

Easing Expectations

*"As a father has compassion on his children,
so the Lord has compassion on those who fear him;
for he knows how we are formed,
he remembers that we are dust."*
Psalm 103:13–14

Glancing anxiously at my watch, I peered down the subway tunnel. "Why is the Metro (Paris subway) so unreliable in the suburbs?" The train finally ambled down the tracks. I climbed in quickly and once again consulted my watch. I could make it, but I would have to run.

Despite my skirt and high heels, I ran from the Metro station to the apartment building where we held our staff meetings. I pushed the doorbell and tried to control my breathing. A final look at my watch relieved my nerves. I had managed, only by the grace of God, to arrive during the eight-minute window.

Expectations for our staff meetings ran high. We could arrive no more than five minutes early or three minutes late. Too early showed a lack of consideration for the host. Too late showed blatant disrespect for the other staff members. This harsh definition of punctuality was only one of many ways my new bosses micromanaged their staff.

A few months earlier I had accepted this position on the ministry staff of a missionary church in Paris, France. The church had limited funds and could only afford a small number of staff members. I wanted to show my appreciation for this honor by excelling in my new position.

I'd worked demanding jobs before, but this one took me by surprise. I didn't seem able to meet the expectations placed on me—which was a first. With hindsight, I realize my mentor in the ministry only seemed to clarify them *after* I failed to meet them. I first learned of the eight-minute window rule when I arrived more than three minutes late to a scheduled meeting. Failing to meet expectations, even the unvoiced ones, resulted in sharp verbal reprimands.

In the beginning, I tried to defend myself by pointing out my unawareness. My mentor shut me down with this simple statement, "Shirley, whenever we are in a disagreement, you should always assume I am right, and you are wrong."

The harshness of this type of leadership didn't necessarily seem wrong to me. My mentor's unrealistic expectations and unkind words actually mirrored my own thought patterns and inner voice. It felt familiar. So instead of defending myself to her again, I took my struggle to God.

Week after week I left our staff meetings and worked my way to my apartment. Once there, I fell on my knees and cried out to God. I begged Him to give me wisdom, so I wouldn't make any more mistakes.

The Acceptance of Unrealistic Expectations

As self-driven achievers, we've learned to accept, and even embrace, the expectations others place on us. Most likely this process began when we were very young. For example, because I knew how to read before I started first grade, my teachers expected me to be a high-achieving student—in every subject.

Sometimes these expectations, even if well intended, were not realistic for us. Still, because of our driven nature and lack of boundaries, we managed to meet them. As we grew, rigid and unrealistic expectations became a normal part of our lives. We easily fell for Satan's lie: *No expectation is unreasonable.* And we built a stronghold that says: *I will push myself relentlessly and meet every expectation.*

Taking them on falls in line with many of the other lies we believed and the strongholds we've built, especially our inclinations to please people and ignore our boundaries. Replacing those lies with God's truths has helped move us toward Spirit-led lives. But because we naturally assume unrealistic expectations, we need to take some time to examine their consequences. It may surprise you, as it did me, what they produce in our hearts and minds.

For years I accepted unrealistic expectations as a way of life. In fact, they didn't even seem unrealistic, just extremely challenging. I scolded myself without mercy whenever I failed to meet any expectation—even an unreasonable one. What I couldn't see was how my frustration in trying to meet them began to shape my inner voice.

The word harsh is defined as excessively critical or negative.[1] And that is exactly how my inner voice sounded. Most people struggle with being their own worst critic. But for self-driven achievers, this inner critic takes on the role of a bully.

If I voiced my thoughts with the tones I heard in my head, my self-talk would border on verbal abuse. I would never dream of speaking to others with the same mean tones and words. But this way of thinking had become normal. It didn't sound wrong when my mentor spoke to me in the same way. But the tyranny of my inner critic didn't only attack my thought patterns—it also affected my actions. I could never let myself off the hook or negotiate for more reasonable expectations.

How about you? Maybe you are beginning to see how unrealistic expectations have given birth to your harsh inner critic. Do people comment that you are too hard on yourself? Can you remember times when you accepted harsh treatment from others? I imagine you can see where your inner critic has pushed you to meet even the most unreasonable expectations.

Negative self-talk and harsh self-criticism feel normal to self-driven achievers. Sometimes we justify them as necessary so we can meet an expectation or goal. Instinctively I knew my self-talk wasn't healthy, but I shrugged it off. "After all," I thought, "I'm only hurting myself." But I couldn't be more wrong. The effects of our inner critic reach farther than ourselves—it spills over into how we treat others.

Why Our Inner Voice Matters

When I struggled under the unkind leadership in Paris, the only solution I could see was to accept and meet the expectations. I prayed for God to change *me*. Instead, He changed my circumstances. New leadership came to oversee the ministry staff. They began to notice, and question, the callousness of the former leaders. As I processed the unjust treatment I had received, the new pastors encouraged me to confront my former mentor.

When I explained how I felt under her leadership, my mentor expressed regret. The tears in her eyes and the distress in her voice conveyed sincere remorse for her harshness. As a result, we were able to achieve reconciliation.

As I look back on that time, I believe she struggled with the same self-driven tendencies as I did. She assumed the full responsibility of making our church membership grow, trying to achieve this result through her efforts. There was so much pressure, and her frustration over not meeting that goal manifested as insensitivity toward herself and those she led.

Jesus teaches this principle, "For the mouth speaks what the heart is full of" (Luke 6:45b). Our words and actions naturally flow out of what is sitting in our hearts. If our hearts are full of criticism and harshness, these are what we will reflect to the world.

During my time in Paris, my frustration spilled out in the way I treated others. My fear of losing relationships prevented me from delivering punitive verbal reprimands. Instead, that aggravation revealed itself through a spirit of meanness.

I easily became impatient under stress. When irritated, I lashed out with a sharp tongue. Although I didn't verbally rebuke people, I often judged them unfairly in my thoughts. Sometimes I wrapped these criticisms in hurtful jokes and apologized when confronted. But I struggled to understand why I harbored such a mean spirit.

How about you? Can you see ways your frustration over meeting unrealistic demands has affected how you think about or treat people? I imagine you, like me, struggle to understand where this harshness comes from—and how to free yourself from it.

Controlling it requires breaking free of the unrealistic expectations we've accepted. To do this, we first need to understand who is ultimately responsible for placing these expectations on us. The answer may surprise us.

Who is Responsible for Our Unrealistic Expectations?

My time in Paris helped me see the inappropriateness of treating others badly. But it did little to change the expectations I had for myself. And I did not change my inner voice. Things finally began to change after a chance conversation with a coworker.

By this time, I had started my new career as an elementary school teacher. Our busy school days left little time to grade and plan lessons, so I did this work on my weekends. When our district set aside a teacher workday, I felt elated. I planned to complete these tasks at school and finally enjoy the weekend. But my heart sank when I read the agenda for the day. Every moment had been filled with mandatory teacher training.

"I really needed a day off this weekend," I sighed to a coworker. "I wish they would give us time to get our other work done."

"If you need a day off," she responded, "give it to yourself." I stared at her in disbelief. I had never before considered the possibility that I could control the expectations I struggled to meet.

Yet here sat my coworker, confident that I not only had the right to ease the expectations placed on me but that it was my responsibility to do so. Her observation gave me pause and then sent me looking for God's wisdom.

I love this gem from the Psalms:

> "As a father has compassion on his children,
>   so the LORD has compassion on those who fear him;
>   for he knows how we are formed,
>   he remembers that we are dust." Psalm 103:13–14

The entire psalm praises God for all His blessings to us. But these verses specifically speak to the expectations God has for us.

The Hebrew word translated as fear in these verses is *yare.*[2] Unlike what we typically think of as fear, this word refers to the reverence or respect we show for people in authority. Throughout the Bible, God sets the expectation for us to revere Him as our *authority.*

Fearing the Lord means more than just respecting Him. It carries the expectation of honoring His kingship through our obedience. And while this is a high standard, the psalm also expresses the *compassion* God has for us. He knows our strengths and weaknesses and graciously makes allowances for them. As a compassionate Father, He doesn't place unrealistic expectations on us. We either accept them from other people, or place them on ourselves.

Does this surprise you? For years I held God ultimately responsible for the unrealistic expectations I felt placed on me. But when we see ourselves as victims of these expectations, we feel powerless to change them. Now that we know the truth, we can begin to ease the ones we've assumed.

As we work to set realistic expectations, we need to balance the same qualities we see in God: *authority and compassion.*

Learning To Set Realistic Expectations

I was hired for my first teaching job just a few days before the start of the school year. Included in my new-hire packet was a long list of items to be completed by the first day of school. It would be a struggle to get it all done, but I accepted the responsibility without question. A few minutes later, I watched another new teacher negotiate the removal of items off the list! Not only did I complete everything, but I also felt angry at her for it. Instead, I should have learned from her example.

This teacher knew how to apply the two keys for easing expectations:

She negotiated with the authorities in her life. Some people have legitimate authority over us, such as supervisors in our workplace. Other expectations come from people who have social authority, such as family members, friends, or coworkers. Because of our drive to achieve, we also place expectations on ourselves.

We've addressed how to ease the expectations of those with social authority in the chapters Aligning Allegiance and Building Boundaries. We are also learning, through the principles outlined in this book, how to ease the expectations we place on ourselves. But negotiating with our supervisors presents a special challenge. We tend to see their authority as fixed and forget that God is sovereign over everyone. This teacher proved to me that we can negotiate with all the authorities in our lives—even our supervisors.

She treated herself with compassion. This teacher showed compassion for herself by correctly assessing both the expectation and her available resources for meeting it. When she realized her limitations, she didn't beat herself up or push herself relentlessly. Instead, she respectfully worked with our principal to reduce her workload.

As self-driven achievers, we tend to take on more than we can comfortably manage. This is because we underestimate the resources needed (time and effort) to meet an expectation. Or we overestimate our supply of resources. We need to make the same allowances for our weaknesses and limitations as God does.

In many ways acknowledging our limitations and weaknesses will remind us of the self-evaluation we completed in the chapter Building Boundaries. But this time our evaluation will help us discern which expectations are unrealistic and will set the stage to negotiate for more reasonable ones.

When I began to apply these two keys, I successfully negotiated deadline extensions, workload reductions, and regularly scheduled work breaks. However, there are situations where negotiating won't work.

If I had refused the harsh expectations placed on me in Paris, I would have had to either quit or face termination. Without a job, I would have been forced to move back to the states. So I chose to stay and suffered the consequences. But the process taught me an important truth about suffering.

Suffering From the Harshness of Others

One story in the Old Testament illustrates this perfectly. The Israelites had emigrated to Egypt under the leadership of Joseph. Although they originally prospered, the time came when a new Egyptian king saw the Israelites as a threat to their nation. Though they had done nothing wrong, the king enslaved them and forced them into harsh labor (Exodus 1:8–14). The Egyptians placed unrealistic expectations on the Israelites and beat them when they failed to meet them (Exodus 5:10–14).

The Israelites could not negotiate for more reasonable demands, so they cried out to God. In response, God chose Moses to lead them out of slavery and to bring them to the promised land (Exodus 6:5–7). In the process, God promised the Israelites, "Then you will know that I am the Lord **your God**, who brought you out from under the yoke of the Egyptians" (Exodus 6:7b *emphasis added*).

Through this narrative, God shows us that sometimes we will suffer from the unjust actions of others. But as God led the Israelites through their suffering, He promised they would experience Him differently. He originally revealed Himself to Moses as "the God of your father, the God of Abraham, the God of Isaac and the God of Jacob" (Exodus 3:6). Through their suffering, God deepened His bond with the Israelites. They would no longer know Him as the God of their ancestors but as their personal God, the One who brought them out from under the yoke of the Egyptians.

The same holds true for us. When we lean on God in our suffering, we will experience Him in a deeper, more personal way. The harsh leadership in Paris drew me closer to God. As He led me through that struggle, He refined my faith. Like the Israelites,

I can look to God as *the Lord my God who rescued me from the yoke of harshness.*

Before we move forward, I'd like to share some personal thoughts. I realize we can experience cruelty in our lives other than in our workplace. I also know it can escalate to violence and threaten our safety. If you are in such a situation, my heart hurts for you. While this type of harshness is outside of the scope of this book, I pray you seek help to protect yourself both physically and emotionally. Please turn to family, friends, spiritual leaders, or professional healthcare providers to receive the support you need.

As we learn to ease our unrealistic expectations, we are well on our way to a Spirit-led life. But we still need to address the ruthless tones of our inner voice.

Replacing Our Harsh Inner Voice with Compassion

As we've seen, the inner voice of a self-driven achiever is harsh and unforgiving. My husband often observes that no one beats me up like I do. Could someone say this about you? The way we talk about ourselves spills out from our critical internal voices. Learning to ease our expectations is a great step toward taming our inner critic. But because our inner voice is so ingrained in critical words and tones, we also need to change the way we talk to ourselves.

The key to this transformation is compassion. But does the idea of being compassionate with yourself feel impossible? The good news is we don't have to learn how to show it to ourselves. We simply have to accept the compassion God has *already given us.* Since He doesn't expect more from us than what we can give, we shouldn't either.

This is obviously easier said than done. Accepting God's love means transforming the way we think. To do this, we need to ignite the power of the Holy Spirit. Here are a couple of spiritual practices that are especially helpful in this process.

Meditating on Scripture: Meditating on God's Word fills our hearts and minds with His truths. Consider the following Scripture:

> "There is no fear in love. But perfect love drives out fear, because fear has to do with punishment. The one who fears is not made perfect in love." 1 John 4:18

The Greek word translated here as fear is *phobos* and it carries the connotation of fleeing in panic, or terror.[3] From John's perspective, God's perfect love cannot coexist with the fear that is tied to punishment. Harshness, on the other hand, *is* linked to punishment. When our thoughts begin sounding like reprimands, harshness has taken root. Without realizing it, we are punishing ourselves for not meeting an expectation.

As we meditate on this verse, we can visualize God's perfect love driving out our punishing thoughts. Sometimes it helps to repeat key phrases like, "There is no fear in love" or "Perfect love drives out fear."

Solitude and silence: It's so important to make time to pull away from all distractions and sit with the Holy Spirit. We can then turn off all the voices that surround us, including our own. As we focus on listening to the Spirit, we can reflect on questions like: Where is this harshness coming from? What expectation have I not met? Was it a reasonable or unreasonable one? Am I trying to punish myself for it? Would God punish me for it? How would God show me compassion in this situation? How can I accept His compassion?

God doesn't place unrealistic expectations on us—He understands our limitations. When we follow His lead, we will ease our expectations and shut the door to harshness.

In place of our self-driven stronghold, we can adopt a new Spirit-led conviction: *I will ease the expectations I place on myself and make them reasonable.* Performancism will lose its grip, and we will be free to experience the Spirit-led life.

Pressing on Toward the Goal

Harshness is not an easy topic to discuss. I imagine the content in this chapter may have surfaced painful memories of how it has impacted your life. Please take time to process these memories with the help of the Holy Spirit. As you pull away from distractions and assume a listening posture, ask Him to help you identify where harshness may be affecting you. Use the following questions as a guide to your reflection:

- What does my self-talk look like? Do I speak to myself with gentleness or harshness?

- In what areas am I trying to do what is unreasonable given my resources, gifts, and circumstances?

- Do I accept harsh treatment from others? If so, what steps can I take to communicate with the aggressor or to step away?

- What are the expectations I am currently working to meet? Are any of them unrealistic? What can I do to make them more reasonable?

Take some time to research additional scriptures that speak to setting realistic expectations. These could be centered on understanding God's expectations for us, His grace and mercy, or on how He makes allowances for our weaknesses and needs.

To get you started, here are a few of my favorites:

- "He has shown you, O mortal, what is good. And what does the LORD require of you? To act justly and to love mercy and to walk humbly with your God." Micah 6:8

- "The simple believe anything, but the prudent give thought to their steps." Proverbs 14:15

- "Prudence is a fountain of life to the prudent, but folly brings punishment to fools." Proverbs 16:22

CHAPTER 8

Cultivating
Collaboration

"Two are better than one,
because they have a good return for their labor."
Ecclesiastes 4:9

Humming happily, I started organizing my new classroom. A move to another city meant letting go of my previous position—teaching at a Christian school. In many ways that had been my dream job. I loved teaching my young students to love Jesus while they also learned to read and write. Our curriculum included scripted lessons for the teachers. It effectively led us through the process of teaching reading. But there wasn't any room to stray from the curriculum and try something new.

So when I accepted my first teaching position in the public school system, I looked forward to unleashing my creativity. I planned on designing the expectations for *my* classroom, writing lesson plans for *my* students, and running everything *my* way. But my dreams came to a crashing halt just a few minutes later when the grade-level team leader invited me to our first collaboration meeting.

"Collaboration meeting?" I remember repeating.

"Oh yes!" she smiled brightly. "Our school district is big on collaboration. Didn't they explain this in your interview?"

Um . . . No, they did not. I think I would have remembered that. Unable to voice my thoughts, I followed her to the meeting place.

That meeting dispelled all hopes of working independently. We would be designing expectations for *our* classrooms, writing lessons for *our* students, and running everything through *our* collaborative efforts.

Disheartened, I left the meeting wondering, "What in the world did I get myself into?"

The Challenges of Working with Others

To collaborate simply means *working together to achieve a common goal.*[1] By this definition, it sounds like a good idea. But for many of us collaboration sounds good in theory, but not in practice. Challenges naturally arise when we ask people with different personalities, opinions, agendas, and professional ethics to work together.

While collaboration challenges everyone, it is especially frustrating for self-driven achievers. By nature, we focus on the end result. Our ability to succeed is threatened when we have to depend on people who may not share that goal or our work ethic. It's easy to believe Satan's lie: *I can only trust myself.* And we build our stronghold which states: *I will work harder in the group to make sure we succeed.*

Our distaste for working with others often starts early—when we were assigned group projects in school. Traditionally everyone in the group received the same grade based on the quality of the end result. Think back to your experiences with this type of group work.

Were you ever put in a group where not everyone cared enough to put in the necessary effort? How did you respond? Did you feel it necessary to micromanage the other members? Or did you do more work to make up for their lack?

On a discussion forum titled "Anyone else hate group projects?",[2] one college student described his experience this way:

> "Bad students love group projects, as long as there is at least one serious student in the group. That is a chance for the goof-offs to get a high grade off the work of serious students."

For self-driven achievers, "bad students" lack the motivation to do what is necessary to earn a high grade. So, as motivated students, we did the bulk of the work, and everyone else profited from our efforts.

In the workplace, collaboration presents different challenges. Coworkers tend to be more motivated, but increased motivation comes with increased passion. Have you ever found yourself in a group of very strong-minded individuals? How did it make you feel? Were you intimidated by their opinions and struggled to share your input? Or if you shared your thoughts, did you find yourself constantly in conflict with the other members? How much extra time did it take to resolve conflicts or convince others of your point of view?

The additional time and energy needed to forge unity in a group of strong-willed individuals can leave us believing the old adage, "Too many cooks spoil the broth." Our frustration leads us to believe that no task can be done well when too many people are involved.

For self-driven achievers, group work often means *more* work. So, it's easy for us to believe that anything we accomplish on our own will be better, and require less time and effort, than anything we do as part of a group. And we cling tightly to our determination to stay independent and self-reliant.

However, there is a reason why my school district, and many other organizations, insist on a collaborative model for the workplace. It can be a powerful tool. God Himself testifies to the positive potential of collaboration.

Understanding God's Perspective on Collaboration

A familiar story from the Old Testament can help us understand God's perspective on collaboration. In the account of the Tower of Babel, we read about people who wanted to build a city and a high tower. But their goals and plans conflicted with God's will. He had asked them to be fruitful and to fill the earth (Genesis 9:1). Instead of honoring God's plan, they wanted to make a name for themselves and settle in one place (Genesis 11:4). God responded by confusing their language so they could no longer work together to achieve their goal.

But let's look at what God specifically observed about their collaborative effort. "If as one people speaking the same language they have begun to do this, then nothing they plan to do will be impossible for them" (Genesis 11:6).

God affirms that when people work together for the same goal, *their potential to achieve is unlimited*. But collaboration isn't just a good idea. God created us to collaborate.

The Bible tells us we are created in the image of God (Genesis 1:26). As such we are meant to bear His image, or essence, to the world. When we think of reflecting His image, attributes like grace or love immediately come to mind. But how often do we think of how God models perfect collaboration by His very nature?

We know He exists in three persons: the Father, the Son, and the Holy Spirit. Yet together they are One. Nothing in our world can serve as a perfect analogy for God's triune nature. But we don't have to fully understand His nature to appreciate the way the three distinct persons work together. They each play a different role, but they work toward the same goal.

We first see their collaboration in the creation of the world. The collective God spoke the world into creation (Genesis 1). But we also see the three distinct persons of God at work. The Spirit hovered over the waters (Genesis 1:2). The apostle Paul affirmed that all things came from the Father (1 Corinthians 8:6). And we know that Jesus was with God in the beginning and nothing was made without Him (John 1:3). We may not fully understand the dynamic, but all three worked together for the common goal of creating this world.

Throughout the Bible, we continue to see them working together, especially in bringing salvation to us. The Father created the plan to send His Son to save us (John 3:16–17). The Holy Spirit anointed Jesus for His ministry (Luke 3:21–22). Finally, Jesus willingly laid down His life for us (John 10:11).

The three persons of God consistently model perfect collaboration. United in purpose, they work together to achieve their goals. Since we are made in their image, we also have been created to collaborate.

As Christians, we know God intends for us to be part of a community of believers. But as self-driven achievers, we struggle to extend this conviction to the workplace. Unlike our church community, all our coworkers may not agree with God's standards for holy living. Yet God promises us we will benefit from collaboration—even in our imperfect workplace.

The Benefits of Collaboration— Even in an Imperfect World

In the book of Ecclesiastes, the author describes two very different workers. The first one, a tireless workaholic, labors by himself. In the end, he is unable to share his success with anyone (Ecclesiastes 4:8).

By contrast, those who learn to work with others receive this promise:

> "Two are better than one, because they have a good return for their labor." Ecclesiastes 4:9

God promises we will receive a good return for our efforts when we work together. In fact, He claims it is better to work with others than by ourselves. Do you find this difficult to believe?

Based on our past experiences, we may have trouble trusting this promise. But when people are willing to collaborate, everyone reaps the benefits. Here are a few ways collaboration can yield a better return for our labor:[3]

- **Greater productivity**: Working with others allows us to multiply our resources and capitalize on our collective strengths.

- **Personal growth**: Every team member brings unique skills and experience to the group. We can grow personally by learning from the other members.

- **Enjoyable work environment**: Collaboration fosters camaraderie which leads to a more enjoyable workplace.

- **Efficient problem-solving**: Each team member brings different problem-solving skills to the group. By working together, solutions can be quickly found and implemented.

- **Creative process**: When people with different skills, perspectives, and experiences come together and brainstorm ideas, they naturally spark creativity in each other.

When I let go of my resistance to collaboration, I began to see its benefits. Through my work with others, I've grown in my ability to handle conflict with diplomacy and tact. I also picked up a few helpful technology skills. Often the members whose perspectives differed the most from mine challenged me to think outside the box.

How about you? As you reflect on your own experiences, can you see ways you grew from working with others? Maybe you learned how to share your thoughts and opinions with greater confidence. Or you picked up a more efficient way to complete your work. Have you experienced camaraderie from collaboration? How do workplace friendships improve your overall job satisfaction?

Collaboration can yield great benefits. But it relies on each member staying committed to the process. When that doesn't happen, it breaks down. But rather than giving up and returning to our self-driven ways, we can lean on God's wisdom and stay faithful to His plan.

Leaning on God's Wisdom
When Collaboration Breaks Down

As self-driven achievers, we know the pain of failed collaboration. It's why we hesitate to embrace it. So, let's look at some ways collaboration breaks down and how God's promises can give us hope.

When groups do not share a common goal or are no longer working together, they are in conflict. It's so easy for us to think conflict impedes progress. But God has a different perspective. "As iron sharpens iron, so one person sharpens another" (Proverbs 27:17).

Ironing out differences is a key part of the collaborative process. Sharing our diverse perspectives and opinions helps us reach stronger and more balanced solutions. We can help facilitate healthy conflict by being "quick to listen, slow to speak and slow to become angry" (James 1:19b).

Sometimes we have to address members who are not fulfilling their responsibilities. In these cases, we can lean on this pearl of wisdom: "A gentle answer turns away wrath, but a harsh word stirs up anger" (Proverbs 15:1). A gentle approach breaks down walls and opens the path for communication.

We can also take confidence in this promise: "When the LORD takes pleasure in anyone's way, he causes their enemies to make peace with them" (Proverbs 16:7). When we seek to please God,

He can bring resolution to any conflict—even with people whose perspectives are completely opposite to ours.

Sometimes collaboration won't work, no matter how hard we try. In these cases, we can stand on this advice from the apostle Paul. "If it is possible, as far as it depends on you, live at peace with everyone" (Romans 12:18). We can rest peacefully knowing we did our best to reach a resolution.

Seeing God's plan for collaboration can be challenging. It takes trust to let go of our independence and self-reliance. We may not be ready to rely on others, but we can start by relying on Him. Let's look at how we can embrace collaboration with the help of the Holy Spirit.

Embracing Collaboration with the Help of the Holy Spirit

For the last several years, our work culture has been steadily moving away from independent and individualistic efforts and toward a collaborative model. While this is in line with God's plan, it does require us to step out of our comfort zones. Here are some practices that can help us engage the Holy Spirit in our process.

We can begin by meditating on this passage:

> "Trust in the LORD with all your heart and lean not on
> your own understanding; in all your ways submit to
> him, and he will make your paths straight."
>
> Proverbs 3:5–6

As we focus on our need to trust God, let's think about times when our own understanding has led us astray. We can envision the path of collaboration becoming straight as we surrender our self-reliant ways to Him.

Next, we can remove ourselves from distractions and sit with the Holy Spirit. As we practice our prayers of surrender, we can release our flawed understanding of collaboration and pray to trust God. We can ask for the power and discipline of the Holy Spirit to help us live in obedience to His plan.

Finally, when we are in the midst of collaboration and begin to feel anxious or frustrated, we can use Ecclesiastes 4:9 as a breath prayer. Breathe in the words: "Two are better than one;" and breathe out the words: "Because they have a good return for their labor."

These spiritual practices will keep us in the presence of God where He transforms our aversion to collaboration. Instead of dreading it, or avoiding it, He will lead us to embrace it. We can let go of our distrust and reluctance to rely on others. Instead, we can adopt a new Spirit-led conviction: *I will embrace collaboration as God intended.*

God never meant for us to be independent and self-reliant. As He leads us through the process, we will learn that we actually do our best work when we work with others. By embracing collaboration, we will continue to loosen the grip performancism has on us. We will no longer be self-driven, but Spirit-led.

Pressing on Toward the Goal

As you learn to trust and embrace God's plan and promise for collaboration, take some time to reflect on the following questions:

- What is my gut reaction to the idea of working with others?

- What fears do I have about collaboration?

- Which of the benefits of collaboration resonate the most with me?

- What steps can I take to help me embrace collaboration?

Find additional Scriptures on God's plan for collaboration. Write out the ones that resonate with you the most.

Here are a few of my favorites:

- "For lack of guidance a nation falls, but victory is won through many advisers." Proverbs 11:14

- "As iron sharpens iron, so one person sharpens another." Proverbs 27:17

- "And whatever you do, whether in word or deed, do it all in the name of the Lord Jesus, giving thanks to God the Father through him." Colossians 3:17

CHAPTER 9

Letting the Spirit Lead

"Since we live by the Spirit, let us keep in step with the Spirit." Galatians 5:25

Glancing around at the expectant, smiling faces gathered at my feet, I opened the book and began to read. A wound-up butterfly, hidden in the pages of the book, suddenly flew out and soared over the heads of my students. Their delighted squeals filled the room. "You see children," I whispered, "reading is magical!"

Story time was always my favorite activity in the classroom. For just a few minutes, my students and I read together for the sheer joy of it. I longed for them to understand how reading can transport us to other places and times. I believed if they experienced the fun of reading, they would persevere and become strong readers.

Even for highly motivated students, learning to read is challenging. In my work in reading instruction, one group of struggling readers took me by surprise. They appeared to be strong readers because they could successfully decode and read books at their grade level. But they could never tell me anything about the passage. Just as I can sometimes correctly read a technical text in French but have no idea what the words mean. In educational circles, we refer to this phenomenon as "word calling." It's where the mind correctly deciphers the letters into words but lacks the ability to create meaning from them.

The missing link between reading words and creating meaning is what we call schema.

As I explained to my young students, schema is the vast collection of everything we have ever heard, seen, felt, or experienced.[1] It houses all our memories. In other words, schema is the lens through which we see the world and interpret information.

The Role Schema Plays in Our Journey to a Spirit-Led Life

With my young charges, sometimes their schema lacked experience with the subject of the text. In those cases, I needed to build their background knowledge so they could understand what they read. This new information then became part of their ever-evolving schema.

Throughout our lives, our schemas continuously evolve and become more robust. As we encounter new information, we may have some background knowledge and experience with the topic. Sometimes that new information conflicts with what resides in our schema. In those situations, we experience cognitive dissonance—the uncomfortable feeling of recognizing two opposing points of view. We then have to choose. We can hold on to the beliefs already housed in our schema. Or we can adopt the new information and allow it to change our schema, and this in turn allows us to view and interpret the world differently.

As self-driven achievers, we have built some (or all) of the strongholds into our schema. These have then influenced how we perceive and interact with the world around us. Each of these strongholds tightens the grip performancism has on our lives. As I shared my personal experiences with these strongholds, I hope you have been able to identify how these strongholds manifest in your life.

Together we have challenged these strongholds with new information from God's Word. Specifically, we've looked at how we can move from self-driven to Spirit-led. This may have given birth to that sense of cognitive dissonance. And with that feeling, comes a choice: Will we hold on to the strongholds that feed our self-driven practices, or will we embrace the freedom promised in God's Word?

Using the following table, let's look back at these strongholds and remind ourselves of the truths found in God's Word.

My prayer is for all of us to adopt these Spirit-led convictions. As we incorporate them into our schema, we will have made the significant first steps toward a Spirit-led life. Let's look a little more closely at what it means to be led by the Spirit.

SELF-DRIVEN STRONGHOLDS	SPIRIT-LED CONVICTIONS
I will build my self-worth and self-confidence through my achievements.	*I will grasp God's grace and love as the determination of my identity and worth and stand with holy confidence.*
I will avoid failure at all costs.	*I will favor failure as an essential part of the learning process.*
I will be successful by focusing solely on my goal.	*I will sift my success by using fair and accurate measurements. The progress toward my goal is just as valuable as the end result.*
I will do whatever is necessary so people will like and accept me.	*I will align myself with Jesus. People will respond to me in the same ways as they did to Him.*
I will ignore my personal needs and boundaries so I can serve others.	*I will build boundaries and trust meeting this God-given need will protect my overall well-being.*
I will push myself relentlessly and meet every expectation.	*I will ease the expectations I place on myself and make them reasonable.*
I will work harder in the group to make sure we succeed.	*I will embrace collaboration as God intended.*

What Does It Mean to Be Led by the Spirit?

Sometimes when we hear the phrase, "led by the Spirit", it invokes the idea of something mysterious or otherworldly. While the work of the Spirit may be a bit mysterious, His purpose is very clear. The Holy Spirit works to accomplish God's will in our lives.

As Christians, we have received salvation through the sacrifice of Jesus. But because we live in this broken world, we still struggle with our sinful desires. The apostle Paul describes how the Spirit helps us in this struggle:

> "So I say, walk by the Spirit, and you will not gratify the desires of the flesh. For the flesh desires what is contrary to the Spirit, and the Spirit what is contrary to the flesh. They are in conflict with each other, so that you are not to do whatever you want. But if you are **led by the Spirit**, you are not under the law." Galatians 5:16–18 (*emphasis added*)

These verses highlight the contrast between the desires of our sinful nature and the moral will of God. As Christians, we no longer live under the requirements of the law. Instead, the Spirit leads us to live godly lives, pleasing to the Lord. Paul reminds us that, "we have been released from the law so that we serve in the new way of the Spirit, and not in the old way of the written code" (Romans 7:6b).

As the Spirit leads us, we will put to death our sinful nature:

> "Therefore, brothers and sisters, we have an obligation—but it is not to the flesh, to live according to it. For if you live according to the flesh, you will die; but

if by the Spirit you put to death the misdeeds of the body, you will live. For those who are led by the Spirit of God are the children of God."

Romans 8:12–14 (*emphasis added*)

It comes down to a question of control. When self-driven, we retain control over our lives and act to satisfy our sinful, performance-driven natures. We create strongholds that drive our self-driven ways. But when Spirit-led, we surrender control and choose to trust the guidance of the Spirit. We dismantle our self-driven strongholds and replace them with God's freedom-giving truths.

The apostle Paul reminds us that living by the Spirit is not a one-and-done deal but a lifetime commitment of matching our steps to those of the Spirit:

"Since we live by the Spirit, let us keep in step with the Spirit." Galatians 5:25

To lead a Spirit-led life, we need to continually surrender our will so we can follow the Lord. The more ingrained the stronghold, the more we will need to work to replace it in our schema. Here are some practical tips to help us keep in step with the Spirit.

Keeping in Step with the Spirit

Practice the spiritual disciplines

When I first became a Christian over forty years ago, I didn't know how to tap into the power of the Holy Spirit. My life became a pattern of holding myself back from doing what's wrong and pushing myself forward to do what's right. I knew

Jesus said His yoke is easy and His burden light (Matthew 11:30), but that isn't how my Christian walk felt.

As I've studied the role of the Holy Spirit in our spiritual formation, I realize we are meant to be in partnership with Him. There are certain spiritual practices we can follow that will keep us in God's presence so He can do the work of transforming us into Christ.

In this book I've shared the ones that have helped me the most with my self-driven strongholds: *scripture meditation, silence, and solitude.* We have practiced these together as we worked to dismantle our self-driven strongholds. I pray these will continue to help you live a Spirit-led life.

Study and meditate on His Word

The apostle Paul wrote these words to the young evangelist, Timothy:

> "All Scripture is God-breathed and is useful for teaching,
> rebuking, correcting and training in righteousness, so
> that the servant of God may be thoroughly equipped
> for every good work." 2 Timothy 3:16–17

The scriptures are the primary way we can know and understand God's will. As we interact with His Word, it trains us to be godly. To keep in step with the Spirit, we need to continuously grow in our knowledge of God's Word.

Together we have studied passages that helped us dismantle our self-driven strongholds. We also practiced meditating on key verses. As we renounced each stronghold, I encouraged you to research and record specific scriptures that resonated with you. Your next steps will be to enhance your knowledge of these scriptures through further Bible study, meditation, or memorization.

Searching our heart through solitude and silence

The scriptures teach us the standard for holy living. We can often see where we have fallen short, but we don't always understand the root cause. Practicing the spiritual disciplines of solitude and silence can help us. It's easier to hear the Spirit when we free ourselves from distractions. He can search our hearts and show us what needs to change. We can also ask Him to help us put to death our sinful natures.

Throughout this book, we have practiced these disciplines in our effort to dismantle our strongholds. Whenever you find yourself returning to your self-driven ways, remember to take time to sit with the Spirit. Ask Him to show you what you need to do to get back on track.

The scriptures are the roadmap for leading godly lives. But some of our situations aren't spelled out in the Bible. God's will isn't always clear when we are considering setting boundaries or choosing which needs to meet. You may wonder, as I did, how the Spirit can help us with these decisions.

The Spirit Helps Us Discern What Is Best

In the apostle Paul's prayer for the Philippians, he asked that their "love may abound more and more in knowledge and depth of insight, so that you [the Philippians] may be able **to discern what is best** and may be pure and blameless for the day of Christ" (Philippians 1:9–10 *emphasis added*).

In situations where what's best can't be discerned simply from the scriptures, we can enlist the help of the Holy Spirit. The practices of solitude and silence can be helpful in these situations. After spending time with the Holy Spirit and asking for guidance, watch and wait for the answer. The Spirit can answer in a variety of ways.

Sometimes we hear the answer through what I think of as Godwinks. This is when two or more events happen in close proximity to each other, and each one points to the same answer. For example, one morning a trusted spiritual friend suggested I submit a devotion for publication on a certain website. As soon as I asked the Spirit for discernment, my pastor sent a text with the same suggestion.

As we're waiting for an answer, we might receive new insights that help us know what to do. These may not come when we're sitting with the Holy Spirit, but after we've returned to our normal, daily tasks. All of a sudden, it's like the light bulb goes on, and we have the answer.

Other times we may feel a persistent urging toward some task or opportunity. For example, several years ago I felt the nudge to start writing. The nudge didn't go away, so I followed the Spirit's guidance and signed up for writing courses. These led to my blog, and eventually to this book.

The Holy Spirit can direct our steps by opening and closing opportunities. He often sends answers through the advice of trusted spiritual mentors. There are also times when the answer comes through a casual conversation with a friend, or a link to a helpful blog post pops up in our social media feed.

Maybe you've had experience with the Spirit's leading. If so, how has He spoken to you? Have you experienced an "aha" moment during your personal study of the Bible? Or can you think of some coincidences in your life that may actually have been Godwinks? Maybe you have felt that internal gentle nudging or heard a distinct inner voice. Other times you may have felt a persistent feeling of discontent which pushed you toward a specific action.

There truly are a variety of ways the Spirit can answer our prayer to discern what is best. But this can feel a little daunting, especially if this is a new practice for us. When we first start leaning in to listen to the Holy Spirit, we may feel haunted by this question: What if I heard wrong? This often comes into play when we have a bias toward a certain course of action. In these cases, we worry that our own voice is telling us what we want to hear. So how can we know if we are truly hearing the voice of the Spirit?

Trusting Ourselves to Follow the Holy Spirit

The apostle John warns us, "Dear friends, do not believe every spirit, but test the spirits to see whether they are from God, because many false prophets have gone out into the world" (1 John 4:1). We are wise to question the messages we hear because the Bible clearly teaches us that there are many false prophets.

The primary way we can test the messages we hear is by comparing them to the Word of God. The Holy Spirit will never prompt us to do something that violates God's commands. But that still leaves a huge gray area. If something isn't clearly against His decrees, how can we know if we are following our voice or that of the Spirit?

Although there are no definitive answers, there are some scriptures that can help us. Look at what Jesus taught:

> "Which of you fathers, if your son asks for a fish, will give him a snake instead? Or if he asks for an egg, will give him a scorpion? If you then, though you are evil, know how to give good gifts to your children, how much more will your Father in heaven give the Holy Spirit to those who ask him!" Luke 11:11–13

If our children ask for food, we would never give them something poisonous like a snake or a scorpion. In the same way, we need to trust that our Father will give us the help of the Holy Spirit when we ask Him for it.

It's true our hearts can deceive us (Jeremiah 17:9). But it's also true that as Christians we became a new creation (2 Corinthians 5:17). This new creation came with a new heart (Ezekiel 36:26). It's always possible that we may hear the Spirit incorrectly. But even in these situations, if we have the heart to do God's will, He can redirect us back to the right path.

Some years ago, a position opened for an Instructional Coach in my school district. I felt the nudge to apply, but it came on the heels of my father's passing. I just didn't have the energy to submit an application. So I ignored the nudging and a coworker received the position. Even though I felt happy for her, I felt a twinge of regret. But I trusted that this position wasn't meant for me.

A few days after the school year started, my coworker had to resign for personal reasons. This time when the position became available, I didn't ignore the Spirit's prompting. Serving as an Instructional Coach was one of my most fulfilling experiences while working in public education.

Learning to listen for the Spirit's direction doesn't come easily. It helps to remember that God sent the Holy Spirit to help us. If God can trust us with His Spirit, then we need to learn to trust ourselves. The more we step out in faith and follow His guidance, the more confident we will become. And as we follow His lead, the Spirit will help us discern what is best.

Final Thoughts

Thank you for taking this journey with me. I pray our time together has helped you recognize your self-driven tendencies and how they impact your life. Like me, I imagine you have found the self-driven life to be exhausting. The term, *led by the Spirit*, sounds so refreshing, and so different from what we experience with our self-driven natures. Even the verbs themselves paint such contrasting pictures.

The verb "to drive" means to frighten or prod something, like cattle, so it moves in a desired direction.[2] This is exactly how it feels when our inner tyrants drive us forward. Propelled by fear, we push ourselves relentlessly toward our goals.

In contrast, "to lead" means to guide, especially by going ahead.[3] Although we may arrive at the same goal, being led has a much gentler connotation. Instead of being pushed from behind, we're inspired to follow the One who leads the way.

As you continually surrender these self-driven strongholds and replace them with God's truths, you will finally be free of your performance-driven nature and able to enjoy the life God has created for you–a life of purpose, minus the angst and inner turmoil. Instead of being a self-driven achiever, you will now enjoy the benefits of a Spirit-led life.

And while you may at times fall back on your self-driven achieving ways, you now have the tools to surrender them again and to continue following the Spirit's guidance. With Jesus as your Shepherd, you will find the freedom you crave. As He promises, "If you hold to my teaching, you are really my disciples. Then you will know the truth, and the truth will set you free" (John 8:31b–32).

Let's imagine someday we make our way back to that quiet and quaint cafe. Sipping our coffee or tea, we sit back and share all the wonderful ways the Lord has led us to freedom.

Live Inspired
Bible Study Companion

To strengthen your understanding of these truths, I've created an additional resource:

Live Inspired: Freeing Ourselves from the Grip of Performancism
Bible Study Companion

This study will guide you to deeper biblical convictions so the Holy Spirit can bring His transformative power into your life. The Bible Study Companion is available at shirleydesmondjackson.com or wherever books are sold.

Acknowledgments

"Every good and perfect gift is from above, coming down from the Father of the heavenly lights."
James 1:17a

Writing, the actual process of putting words on a page, is a solitary endeavor. But it takes a community to take those pages, publish them, and make them known to readers. I have so many to thank.

First of all, I'm so grateful for my husband, Mark, who has given me the time, space, and resources to pursue this dream. He not only supported me as I wrote this book, but he also walked beside me as I experienced many of the lessons I share in its pages. Thank you for your midnight runs to the post office on those crazy April 15 nights, for helping me set up (and take down) my classroom each year, and for listening to my early writing drafts. Your steadfast nature perfectly balances my self-driven achiever personality. I'm so thankful I could lean on your calming strength through all of life's ups and downs. You truly are my better half. We're still having fun, and you're still the one!

Next, a huge thank you to my children: Kendra, Daniel, and Katia. I've learned so much from being your mom. Because of you I finally understood what it means to love unconditionally. I love you all to the moon and back, and then some. Thank you for filling my life with joy. I love the adults you have become (even if I still miss the time when you were kids). Keep following your passions and loving life—you inspire me!

Kudos to Buddy, my father-in-law, who allowed us to turn his life and house inside out and upside down when we moved to Virginia. Thank you for cheering me on in my writing projects.

A big shout out to my two close friends: Jody Rohleder and Teresa Linner. These two women have been by my side for many of the experiences noted in this book. Thank you for helping me keep a spiritual perspective and finding strength in God during the tough times. You believed in me when I didn't believe in myself. Without you and your friendship, this book would not have been written.

I am deeply indebted to Benjamin and Melina Hutchins who trained me in the spiritual disciplines. Because of your training, I learned how to access the transformative power of the Holy Spirit. I will be forever grateful to both of you.

The community at COMPEL Training will always have a special place in my heart. I would never have become a writer if not for this incredible ministry. I'm grateful for the insightful training, publishing opportunities, friends, and support you have given me. You helped me find and then refine my writing voice.

Mindy Kiker and Jennifer Kochert and the Flourish Academy Community—thank you! Your practical classes and coaching calls provided the necessary steps to organize and publish this book. I can't thank you enough for the invaluable counsel you provide.

Many thanks to my COMPEL Critique Group members—Margaret, Carmella, Joy, Linda (1), Rachel, Linda (2), Michelle, and Joanna.

Your critiques make me a stronger writer. Thank you for lending your insights and wisdom to several chapters of this book. I value your input, both as writers and as fellow teachers of God's Word.

For my first ever focus group: Allie, Briana, Cat, Jeannette, Jenni, Jody, Kat, Kendra, Margaret, Sarah, Sheila, Shelby, Tabitha, and Teresa: a thousand thanks for partnering with me on this book project! Having you on board kept me motivated and on track. Your feedback provided the information I needed to make sure this book would meet people's needs. You exhibited collaboration at its best. Thank you!

I'm so appreciative for Melanie Chitwood who edited the first edition of this book. From the very beginning you expressed a desire to make this book the best it could be. Thank you for praying over this book and for our partnership.

Through a number of events, the Holy Spirit led me to work with Mandy Roberson and the team at Market Refined Media & Publishing. They have truly been instrumental in bringing this second edition to life. I appreciate their wisdom, integrity, and professionalism. I'm so blessed to work with such an incredible group of people.

A huge component of the MRM team is Carey Scott who edited this second edition. I love your insights, encouragement, and constructive criticisms. You not only made this book better; you helped me grow as a writer. Thank you for sharing your expertise with me!

Of course, none of this would be possible without the saving grace of Jesus. Over forty years ago, God sent a Christian and professional woman, Nancy, into my workplace. Her exemplary life became the first Bible I ever read. Her unwavering joy attracted me to her church, and ultimately to Jesus. She taught me the importance of modeling Jesus in our workplaces. I will be eternally grateful for her friendship.

Finally, I thank you, my readers. Of all the books available, you chose to spend your time and energy on this one. I am grateful for your readership and pray the lessons He taught me will bless your life as well.

God never ceases to amaze me with His good and perfect gifts.

About the Author

Prompted by gratitude, Shirley Desmond Jackson loves to teach others the truths found in God's Word. Her driving passion is to help women connect with an extraordinary God who meets us in the middle of our ordinary lives. After serving on the foreign mission field in Paris, France, she married her best friend, Mark. Together they raised three children and now shepherd the Married Ministry of their church. In her free time, she loves to spend time with family—especially her two precious grandchildren.

For more Bible lessons and materials, connect with Shirley on her website at shirleydesmondjackson.com. You can also find her on Facebook and Instagram.

Endnotes

Chapter 1

1   Wordhippo.com, s.v. "self-driven (adj.)", accessed August 9, 2024, https://www.wordhippo.com/what-is/another-word-for/self-driven.html

2   BibleHub.com, s.v. "dunamis (n.)," accessed March 29, 2022, https://biblehub.com/greek/1411.htm

3   BibleHub.com, s.v., "agape (n.)," accessed June 7, 2024, https://biblehub.com/greek/26.htm

4   BibleHub.com, s.v., "sóphronismos (n.)," accessed June 7, 2024, https://biblehub.com/greek/4995.htm

Chapter 2

1 BibleHub.com, s.v., "lutroó (v.)," accessed June 14, 2024, https://biblehub.com/greek/3084.htm

2   Biblehub.com, s.v. "charis (n.)," accessed February 4, 2022, https://biblehub.com/greek/5485.htm

3   Dictionary.com, s.v., "gift (n.)," accessed February 4, 2022, https://www.dictionary.com/browse/gift

4   Krysta D'Costa, "The Obligation of Gifts: For those of you with Christmas trees, they probably look a little barren following the unwrapping of presents. What did you get for Christmas?," Anthropology in Practice, Scientific America, December 26, 2014, https://blogs.scientificamerican.com/anthropology-in-practice/the-obligation-of-gifts/#:~:text=Gifts%20should%20be%20offered%3B%20they,in%20the%20obligation%20to%20receive

5   Neil Coffee, "gifts and giving, Roman," Oxford Classical Dictionary, December 19, 2017, https://oxfordre.com/classics/classics/abstract/10.1093/acrefore/9780199381135.001.0001/acrefore-9780199381135-e-8239?rskey=sUK11f&result=1

6   Daniel K. Eng, "What a Patron We Have In Jesus: What Greco-Roman Patronage Teaches Us About Friendship with Jesus," The Gospel Coalition, December 25, 2021, https://www.thegospelcoalition.org/article/patron-have-jesus/

Chapter 3

1   "Carol Dweck, Lewis and Virginia Eaton Professor of Psychology, Stanford University," Edutopia, accessed April 7, 2022, https://www.edutopia.org/profile/carol-dweck

2   Jennifer Smith, "Growth Mindset vs Fixed Mindset: How what you think affects what you achieve," Mindset Health, September 25, 2020, https://www.mindsethealth.com/matter/growth-vs-fixed-mindset

Chapter 4

1   Merriam-webster.com, s.v., "failure (n.)," accessed June 15, 2024, https://www.merriam-webster.com/dictionary/failure

2   Dictionary.com, s.v., "success (n.)," accessed January 24, 2022, https://www.dictionary.com/browse/success

3   "As You Climb the Ladder of Success, Be Sure It's Leaning Against the Right Building: Stephen R. Covey? Thomas Merton? Allen Raine? Anna Adaliza Evans? Mae Maloo? H. Jackson Brown? Sarah Francis Brown? Anonymous?," Quote Investigator, August 17, 2017, https://quoteinvestigator.com/2017/08/17/ladder/

Chapter 5

1   Shauna Reid, "4 questions for Mitch Prinstein: The UNC-Chapel Hill director of clinical psychology offers insights on how popularity in adolescence-or a lack of it-shapes people's lives," American Psychological Association 48, no. 8, September 2017, https://www.apa.org/monitor/2017/09/conversation-prinstein

2   Ibid.

3   Stephen Spencer, "The Secret To Success Is Likeability Rather Than High Status with Mitch Prinstein," Get Yourself Optimized, June 14, 2018, https://www.getyourselfoptimized.com/secret-to-success-is-likeability-rather-than-high-status-mitch-prinstein/

4   Ibid.

5   "What can we learn from Jesus' feeding of the 5,000?," Got Questions, accessed October 7, 2021, https://www.gotquestions.org/feeding-the-5000.html

6   Richard Niell Donovan, "Biblical Commentary (Bible Study) Acts 7:55-60," Sermon Writer, accessed June 22, 2024, https://sermonwriter.com/biblical-commentary-old/acts-755-60/

Chapter 6

1   "Here's What Happens When You Don't Get Enough Sleep (and How Much You Really Need a Night,' Cleveland Clinic, March 25, 2022, https://health. clevelandclinic.org/happens-body-dont-get-enough-sleep/

2   Ibid.

3   Richard Niell Donovan, "Biblical Commentary (Bible Study) Matthew 11:16-19, 25-30," Sermon Writer, accessed November 1, 2021, https://sermonwriter.com/ biblical-commentary-old/matthew-1116-19-25-30/

4   BibleHub.com, s.v. "shabath (v.)," accessed November 1, 2021, https://biblehub. com/hebrew/7673a.htm

5   BibleHub.com, s.v. "anapauó (v.)," accessed November 1, 2021, https:// biblehub.com/greek/373.htm

6   "Here's What Happens When You Don't Get Enough Sleep (and How Much You Really Need a Night,' Cleveland Clinic, March 25, 2022, https://health. clevelandclinic.org/happens-body-dont-get-enough-sleep/

7   Rhett Power, "A Day of Rest: 12 Scientific Reasons It Works: Most major religions call for a day of rest...science agrees," Inc., Accessed November 1, 2021, https://www.inc.com/rhett-power/a-day-of-rest-12-scientific-reasons-it-works.html

8   "Here's What Happens When You Don't Get Enough Sleep (and How Much You Really Need a Night,' Cleveland Clinic, March 25, 2022, https://health. clevelandclinic.org/happens-body-dont-get-enough-sleep/

9   Rhett Power, "A Day of Rest: 12 Scientific Reasons It Works: Most major religions call for a day of rest...science agrees," Inc., Accessed November 1, 2021, https://www.inc.com/rhett-power/a-day-of-rest-12-scientific-reasons-it-works.html

10   Kat Boogaard, "What is Parkinson's Law and why is it sabotaging your productivity?," Work Life, February 12, 2022, Accessed June 28, 2024, https://www. atlassian.com/blog/productivity/what-is-parkinsons-law#:~:text=What%20 is%20Parkinson's%20Law%3F,%E2%80%9CThe%20Economist%E2%80%9D%20 in%201955.

11   BibleHub.com, s.v. "phortion (n.)," accessed November 1, 2021, https:// biblehub.com/greek/5413.htm

12   BibleHub.com, s.v., "baros (n.)," accessed November 1, 2021, https:// biblehub.com/greek/922.htm

Chapter 7

1 Merriam-webster.com, s.v., "harsh" (adj.)," accessed April 9, 2022, https://www.merriam-webster.com/dictionary/harshness

2 BibleHub.com, s.v., "yare" (v.), accessed June 28, 2024, https://biblehub.com/hebrew/3372a.htm

3 BibleHub.com, s.v., "phobos" (v.), accessed June 28, 2024, https://biblehub.com/greek/5401.htm

Chapter 8

1 Dictionary.com, s.v., "collaborate" (v.). accessed July 5, 2024, https://www.dictionary.com/browse/collaborate

2 r/college, "Anyone else hate group projects?" *Reddit*, November 23, 2022, https://www.reddit.com/r/college/comments/z2u6w8/anyone_else_hate_group_projects/

3 Madeline Miles, "13 Benefits of collaboration your organization needs to know," BetterUp, August 1, 2023, Accessed August 13, 2024, https://www.betterup.com/blog/benefits-of-collaboration

Chapter 9

1 Kendra Cherry, "The Role of a Schema in Psychology," Very Well Mind, last updated September 23, 2019, https://www.verywellmind.com/what-is-a-schema-2795873

2 Merriam-Webster.com, s.v., "drive (v.)," accessed April 10, 2022, https://www.merriam-webster.com/dictionary/drive

3 Merriam-Webster.com, s.v., "lead (v.)," accessed April 10, 2022, https://www.merriam-webster.com/dictionary/lead

Notes